Recipes
American Cooking: The Eastern Heartland

Contents

Introductory Notes 2
Soups 8
Vegetables and Salads .17
Meat 28
Poultry and Game Birds 45
Fish and Shellfish 62
Breads, Biscuits and Breakfast Cakes 80
Pickles, Preserves and Relishes 103
Nuts 111
Desserts 114
Cookies 145
Recipe Index 151

Illustrations:
Homemade Egg Noodles 4
Pasties, Michigan Style 30
Half-Moon Cake Pan 135

Foods of the World

TIME-LIFE BOOKS, NEW YORK

Introductory Notes

Atlantic Clams

Two types of Atlantic clams are important foods: the soft-shell, or long-necked, clam *(Mya arenaria)* and the hard-shell, called littleneck on the Pacific Coast, clam *(Venus mercenaria)*. Both are roughly oval in shape, the hard-shell clam nearly round. The soft clam has a thin, brittle shell and a distinctive long siphon, or neck; the hard clam has a thick, solid shell and a short neck. Hard clams are frequently served raw on the half shell; soft clams are always cooked before they are eaten.

Though any soft clam may be steamed successfully, Easterners consider the small ones—under 2 inches in length—best and refer to these as steamer clams.

The hard clam is usually referred to by its old Indian name, quahog (pronounced "co-hog"). Confusingly, some clammers differentiate between hard clams on the basis of their size, using the term quahog only for a big clam that may be 4 to 5 inches long. They call the medium-sized, 2½- to 3-inch clam a cherrystone, and the small 1½- to 2-inch clam is known as a littleneck.

Soft-shell clams are most plentiful north of Cape Cod but can be dug as far south as Cape Hatteras. The same variety was accidentally introduced to the Pacific Coast about 1880 by being mixed with shipments of young Eastern oysters, and the soft clams now thrive along the shoreline from San Francisco to British Columbia.

Quahogs are found all along the Atlantic Coast from Canada south, and in the Gulf of Mexico. Related members of the *Venus* genus, locally known as butter clams and littleneck clams, are found on Pacific beaches from California to Alaska.

The surf clam *(Spisula solidissima),* which occurs from Labrador to South Carolina, is a large heavy species with tougher meat than the quahog; it goes by such names as sea clam, hen clam and chowder clam. Though not widely popular, it is sometimes substituted for the quahog in chowders and at clambakes.

Clams, mussels and oysters are sold to markets and restaurants by licensed fishermen and come from numbered beds, and the chance of encountering shellfish from polluted waters is slight. Amateurs should check with local authorities to make sure that the waters where they go for shellfish are unpolluted. (By law, polluted areas closed to fishing must be posted.) Clams that are not tightly closed when dug must not be eaten.

How to Prepare and Seal Canning Jars

To ensure consistent results in home canning, use standard canning jars or jelly glasses with matching lids. Examine each jar or glass carefully and discard those with covers that do not fit securely and those with cracked or chipped edges. An airtight seal is essential to prevent spoilage.

Wash the jars, glasses, lids and rings in hot, soapy water and rinse them in scalding water. Place them in a large deep pot and pour in enough hot water to cover them completely. Bring to a boil over high heat, then turn off the heat while you finish cooking the food that you plan to can. The jars or glasses must be hot when they are filled.

To prepare to seal the glasses, grate a 4-ounce bar of paraffin into the top of a double boiler (preferably one with a pouring spout), and melt the paraffin over hot water.

When the food is ready for canning, lift the jars or glasses from the pot with tongs and stand them upright on a level surface. Leave the lids and rings in the pot until you are ready to use them. Fill and seal the jars one at a time, filling each jar to within ⅛ inch of the top or each glass to within ½ inch of the top. Each jar should be sealed quickly and tightly with its ring and lid. (If there is not enough food to fill the last jar or glass completely, do not attempt to seal it. Refrigerate and use the food within the next week.)

Jelly glasses also should be sealed at once. Pour a single thin layer of hot paraffin over the surface, making sure it covers the jelly completely and touches all sides of the glass. If air bubbles appear on the paraffin, prick them immediately with the tip of a knife. Let the glasses rest until the paraffin cools and hardens, then cover with metal lids.

If a recipe calls for finishing the preserving process with a water bath, place the filled and sealed jars side by side on a rack in a canner or other deep large pot. Pour in enough hot (not boiling) water to immerse the jars by at least 1 inch, securely cover the pot with its lid, and bring to a boil over moderate heat. Boil for the time recommended. Then, with tongs, remove the jars from the pot and let them cool for about 12 hours. Test the seal of ring-top lids by pressing the center of the top of each lid with your forefinger. If the flat inner lid remains in place, unscrew the outer ring, leaving the seal intact. If the inner lid moves, the jar is not properly sealed; refrigerate and serve the food within a week.

For additional information on canning, see "How to Make Jellies, Jams and Preserves at Home," USDA Home and Garden Bulletin No. 56, and "Making Pickles and Relishes at Home," USDA Home and Garden Bulletin No. 92. These bulletins cost 15 cents each and can be ordered from Superintendent of Documents, U.S. Government Printing Office, Washington, D.C. 20402.

1 Make a well in a mound of flour, break in three eggs and add the water.

2 Push the flour in from the edges and gradually incorporate it into the eggs.

5 Whisk away any excess flour from the surface of the dough with a pastry brush.

6 Roll the dough out almost paper thin, turning it about 2 inches after each roll.

Homemade Egg Noodles

To make about 1 pound

2 to 2½ cups unsifted flour	3 eggs
½ teaspoon salt	1 tablespoon cold water

Combine 2 cups of the flour and the salt in a deep bowl or in a heap on a pastry board. Make a well in the center and add the eggs and water. With your fingers or a spoon, gradually mix the dry ingredients into the liquid ones. When the mixture is well blended, gather it into a ball.

Knead the dough on a board as shown above, or in the bowl, by pushing it down with the heels of your hands, pressing it forward and folding it back on itself. As you knead, incorporate up to ½ cup more flour, sprinkling it over the ball by the tablespoonful and adding only enough to make a firm dough. Knead for about 10 minutes in all.

Gather the dough into a ball, place it on a floured board or table and,

4

3 Collect the particles of flour with a scraper and gather the dough into a ball.

4 Knead the dough for 10 minutes: push it down, forward, and then back on itself.

7 Trim the edges and cut 2-inch potpie squares with a pastry wheel or small knife.

8 Or trim the edges and cut the dough into long noodles each about ¼ inch wide.

with the heel of your hand, press it into a circle about 1 inch thick. Dust a little flour over and under it and roll it out from the center to within an inch of the far edge. Lift the dough and turn it about 2 inches; roll again from the center to the far edge.

Repeat—lifting, turning, rolling—until the circle is almost paper thin. If the dough sticks to the board or table, lift it gently with a metal spatula and sprinkle a little flour under it.

To make potpie squares *(page 47)*, cut the dough into 2-inch squares with a small sharp knife or a pastry wheel. Place the squares in one layer on a piece of wax paper. To make egg noodles, slice the dough into ¼-inch-wide strips with a pastry wheel or long sharp knife.

The freshly made potpies or noodles may be cooked at once or covered tightly with plastic wrap and kept in the refrigerator for a day or so or in the freezer for several months.

Short-Crust Pastry

To make one 9-inch pastry shell or
 piecrust top

NONSWEET SHORT-CRUST PASTRY
6 tablespoons unsalted butter,
 chilled and cut into ¼-inch bits
2 tablespoons lard, chilled and cut
 into ¼-inch bits
1½ cups unsifted flour
1 teaspoon salt
3 to 4 tablespoons ice water

SWEET SHORT-CRUST PASTRY
6 tablespoons unsalted butter,
 chilled and cut into ¼-inch bits
2 tablespoons lard, chilled and cut
 into ¼-inch bits
1½ cups unsifted flour
¼ teaspoon salt
1 tablespoon sugar
3 to 4 tablespoons ice water

TO PREPARE THE PASTRY DOUGH: In a large, chilled bowl, combine the butter and lard bits, the flour and salt. (Add 1 tablespoon of sugar, if you are making a sweet pastry.) With your fingertips, rub the flour and fat together until the mixture looks like flakes of coarse meal.

Pour 3 tablespoons of ice water over the mixture all at once, toss together lightly and gather the dough into a ball. If the dough crumbles, add up to 1 tablespoon more ice water by drops until the particles adhere. Dust the pastry dough with a little flour and wrap it in wax paper. Refrigerate for at least 1 hour before using.

TO MAKE AN UNFILLED PIE SHELL: Spread 1 tablespoon of softened butter over the bottom and sides of a 9-inch pie pan with a pastry brush.

On a lightly floured surface, pat the chilled short-crust pastry dough into a rough circle about 1 inch thick. Dust a little flour over and under it, and roll it out from the center to within an inch of the far edge of the circle. Lift the dough and turn it clockwise about 2 inches; roll again from the center to within an inch or so of the far edge. Repeat—lifting, turning, rolling—until the circle is about ⅛ inch thick and 13 to 14 inches in diameter. If the dough sticks to the board or table, lift it gently with a metal spatula and sprinkle a little flour under it. Drape the dough over the rolling pin, lift it up, and unroll it slackly over the buttered pie pan. Gently press the dough into the bottom and sides of the pan, taking care not to stretch it. With a pair of scissors, cut off the excess dough from the edges, leaving a 1-inch overhang all around the outside rim. Tuck the overhang under the edge all around and crimp it with your fingers or the tines of a fork.

TO MAKE A PARTIALLY BAKED PIE SHELL: Preheat the oven to 400°. Roll out the short-crust pastry dough as described above and fit it into a buttered 9-inch pie pan. To prevent the pie shell from buckling as it bakes, spread a piece of buttered aluminum foil across the pan and press it gently into the bottom and against the sides of the pie shell. Bake in the middle of the oven for 10 minutes, then remove the foil. Bake for another 2 or 3 minutes, or until the pastry is a very delicate golden color. Remove the pie shell from the oven and cool to room temperature before filling.

TO MAKE A FULLY BAKED PIE SHELL: Preheat the oven to 400°. Roll out the short-crust pastry dough as described above and fit it into a buttered 9-inch pan. To prevent the pie shell from buckling as it bakes, spread a piece of buttered aluminum foil across the pan and press it gently into the bottom and against the sides of the pie shell. Bake in the middle of the oven for 10 minutes, then remove the foil. Bake for 4 or 5 minutes longer, or until the pastry is lightly browned. Remove the pie shell from the oven and cool to room temperature before filling.

Homemade Mayonnaise

To make about 2 cups

3 egg yolks, at room temperature
1 to 3 teaspoons strained fresh
   lemon juice
½ teaspoon dry mustard
½ teaspoon salt

⅛ teaspoon ground white pepper
1½ cups vegetable or olive oil or
   a combination of both
2 tablespoons boiling water
   (optional)

Warm a small mixing bowl in hot water, dry it quickly but thoroughly, and drop in the egg yolks. With a wire whisk or a rotary or electric beater, beat the yolks vigorously for about 2 minutes, until they thicken and cling to the beater when it is lifted from the bowl. Stir in 1 teaspoon of the lemon juice, the mustard, salt and white pepper.

Beat in ½ cup of the oil, ½ teaspoon at a time; make sure each addition is absorbed before adding more. By the time ½ cup of the oil has been beaten in, the sauce should be the consistency of thick cream. Pour in the remaining oil in a thin stream, beating constantly. Taste for seasoning and add up to 2 more teaspoonfuls of lemon juice if desired.

To make the mayonnaise creamier and lessen the danger of separating, beat in the boiling water, 1 tablespoon at a time. Cover the mayonnaise tightly with foil or plastic wrap and refrigerate until ready to use. The mayonnaise can safely be kept in the refrigerator for up to one week.

SOUPS

Wild Elderberry Soup

To serve 4

3 cups wild elderberries
1 to 1½ quarts water
½ cup sugar

2 teaspoons cornstarch combined
   with 2 teaspoons water
1 to 3 teaspoons strained fresh
   lemon juice (optional)

Wash the berries in a sieve or colander under cold running water and pick out and discard any that are badly blemished. Place the berries in a 2- to 3-quart enameled or stainless-steel saucepan, pour in 1 quart of water and bring to a boil over high heat. Reduce the heat to low and simmer partially covered for about 45 minutes, or until the berries are soft and can be easily mashed against the sides of the pan with the back of a spoon.

Rub the elderberries through a fine sieve with the back of a large spoon, or press the juice and pulp through a food mill into a deep bowl. Discard the seeds and skins. Measure the elderberry juice and add enough water to make 1 quart.

Return the liquid to the saucepan, add the sugar and, stirring constantly, bring to a simmer over moderate heat. Still stirring, pour in the cornstarch mixture and simmer until the soup thickens lightly and is smooth. Taste and add the lemon juice if desired. Serve at once, accompanied, if you like, by sour cream.

NOTE: Wild grapes, blackberries, rum cherries, or huckleberries (or any combination of these fruits) may be substituted for the wild elderberries. Additional sugar may be necessary depending on the tartness of the berries.

Shaker Potato-Leek Soup

To serve 6 to 8

1 quart water
6 medium-sized boiling potatoes, scrubbed but not peeled
1½ teaspoons caraway seeds
1½ teaspoons salt
3 medium-sized leeks, including 2 inches of the trimmed green tops, cut lengthwise in half, thoroughly washed and finely chopped
3 slices lean bacon
2 cups milk
1 teaspoon crumbled dried marjoram
½ teaspoon paprika
⅛ teaspoon ground white pepper

In a heavy 4- to 5-quart casserole, bring the water to a boil over high heat. Add the potatoes, caraway seeds and salt, and cook briskly for about 20 minutes, or until the potatoes show only slight resistance when pierced with the point of a small sharp knife. With a slotted spoon, transfer the potatoes to a plate, and reserve the cooking liquid. Peel and chop the potatoes fine, stir them into the cooking liquid, add the leeks and bring to a boil over high heat. Reduce the heat to low and simmer the soup partially covered for 30 minutes.

Meanwhile, place the bacon in a heavy 8- to 10-inch ungreased skillet and fry it over moderate heat. Turn the slices with tongs until they are crisp and brown and have rendered all their fat. Then drain the bacon on paper towels, crumble it into bits and set it aside.

Purée the soup through the coarsest blade of a food mill or, with the back of a spoon, rub it through a coarse sieve set over a bowl. Return the soup to the casserole and with a whisk stir in the milk, marjoram, paprika and pepper. Taste and add more salt if necessary. Whisking occasionally, simmer the soup over moderate heat until it is heated through.

Ladle the potato-leek soup into a heated tureen or individual soup plates, sprinkle the bacon bits on top and serve at once.

Philadelphia Pepper Pot

To serve 6

1 pound tripe, cut into ½-inch
   cubes
A meaty veal shank (about 1
   pound), sawed into 2 or 3 pieces
2 quarts water
4 to 6 whole black peppercorns
1 teaspoon salt
4 tablespoons butter

1 cup finely chopped onions
½ cup finely chopped celery
½ cup finely chopped green pepper
3 tablespoons flour
2 medium-sized boiling potatoes,
   peeled and cut into ¼-inch dice
Crushed dried hot red pepper
Freshly ground black pepper

Combine the tripe, veal shank and water in a heavy 4- to 5-quart cas-serole. The water should cover the meats by at least 2 inches; if necessary add more. Bring to a boil over high heat, meanwhile skimming off the foam and scum as they rise to the surface. Add the peppercorns and salt, reduce the heat to low, and simmer partially covered for 2 hours, or until the tripe is tender.

With a slotted spoon, transfer the tripe and pieces of veal shank to a platter or cutting board. Remove the veal from the shank, discard the bones and cut the meat into ½-inch pieces. Strain the cooking liquid through a fine sieve set over a bowl; measure and reserve 6 cups. If there is less, add enough water to make that amount.

In the same 4- to 5-quart casserole, melt the butter over moderate heat. When the foam subsides, add the onions, celery and green pepper and stir for about 5 minutes. When the vegetables are soft but not brown, add the flour and mix well. Stirring constantly, pour in the reserved cook-ing liquid in a slow, thin stream and cook over high heat until the soup thickens lightly, comes to a boil and is smooth. Add the potatoes, tripe and veal, reduce the heat to low, cover partially, and simmer for 1 hour.

Taste for seasoning. Add more salt if needed and enough crushed red pepper and freshly ground black pepper to give the soup a distinctly pep-pery flavor. Serve at once from the casserole or in individual soup plates.

Philadelphia Snapper Soup

To serve 6 to 8

2½ pounds snapping-turtle meat, thoroughly defrosted if frozen, cut into 2-inch pieces
1½ cups flour
1 teaspoon salt
½ teaspoon freshly ground black pepper
½ pound lean salt pork, trimmed of all rind, the pork cut into ¼-inch dice

1 cup finely chopped onions
½ cup finely chopped celery
½ cup finely chopped carrot
1 teaspoon finely chopped garlic
1 quart beef stock, fresh or canned
2 tablespoons tomato paste
1 medium-sized bay leaf, finely crumbled
½ teaspoon crumbled dried thyme
1 cup water (optional)
2 tablespoons dry Madeira

Pat the snapper meat completely dry with paper towels. Then combine the flour, salt and pepper in a paper bag, add the snapper pieces and shake vigorously to coat all sides evenly. Remove the meat from the bag and, one piece at a time, shake off the excess flour.

In a heavy 4- to 5-quart casserole, fry the pork dice over moderate heat until it is crisp and brown and has rendered all its fat. Transfer the dice to paper towels to drain. Brown the snapper 4 or 5 pieces at a time in the fat remaining in the pan. Turn the pieces frequently with a slotted spoon and regulate the heat so that they color richly and evenly without burning. As they brown, transfer them to a plate.

Pour off all but about 3 tablespoons of the fat from the pan and add the onions, celery, carrot and garlic. Stir over moderate heat until the vegetables are soft but not brown. Stir in the beef stock, tomato paste, bay leaf, thyme and reserved pork bits. Bring to a boil over high heat and add the snapper and the liquid that has accumulated around it.

Reduce the heat to low and simmer partially covered for 2 hours, or until the snapper is tender and shows no resistance when pierced with the point of a small sharp knife. Check the pan from time to time and regulate the heat to keep the soup at a gentle simmer. Add up to 1 cup of water if the liquid cooks away too rapidly.

Stir in the Madeira, taste for seasoning, and serve the snapper soup from a heated tureen.

Consommé Bellevue

To serve 6 to 8

4 cups chicken stock, fresh or
   canned, thoroughly skimmed of
   all surface fat
2 cups fresh clam broth *(see steamer
   clams remoulade, page 71)*, or

substitute 2 cups bottled clam
   juice
A pinch of ground hot red pepper
   (cayenne)
¼ cup heavy cream, chilled

This ingenious blend of chicken and clam broths was first devised more than 50 years ago by a chef at the Bellevue Stratford Hotel in Philadelphia —where it is still a proudly served specialty.

Combine the chicken stock, clam broth and red pepper in a heavy 2- to 3-quart saucepan and bring to a boil over high heat. Reduce the heat to low, cover partially, and simmer for 15 minutes.

    Meanwhile, in a chilled bowl, whip the cream with a wire whisk or a rotary or electric beater until it is stiff enough to stand in unwavering peaks on the beater when it is lifted from the bowl.

    Taste the consommé for seasoning, then ladle it into heated individual soup plates. Float a tablespoonful of whipped cream on the surface of each portion and serve at once.

Shaker Herb Soup

To serve 4 to 6

4 tablespoons butter
1 cup finely chopped celery
3 tablespoons finely cut fresh chives
4 tablespoons finely cut fresh sorrel,
   or substitute 2 tablespoons
   bottled or canned sorrel
1 tablespoon crumbled dried chervil

1 teaspoon crumbled dried tarragon
1 quart chicken stock, fresh or
   canned
Freshly ground black pepper
Ground nutmeg, preferably freshly
   grated
1 cup freshly grated Cheddar cheese

In a heavy 2- to 3-quart saucepan, melt the butter over moderate heat. When the foam begins to subside, add the celery and chives and, stirring frequently, cook for about 5 minutes, until they are soft but not brown. Stir in the sorrel, chervil and tarragon and cook for a minute. Then add the chicken stock and a few grindings of pepper and bring the soup to a boil over high heat. Reduce the heat to low and simmer partially covered for 20 minutes.

Taste for seasoning, ladle the soup into individual heated bowls, and sprinkle each portion with a little nutmeg. Serve at once, accompanied by a bowl of grated cheese.

Clam Bisque
To serve 6

3 dozen hard-shell clams *(see page 2)*, each about 3 inches in diameter, shucked (about 3 cups), with their liquor reserved
4 tablespoons butter

¼ cup flour
¼ teaspoon crumbled dried thyme
¼ teaspoon freshly ground black pepper
2 cups light cream

Put the clams through the finest blade of a meat grinder, or purée them in an electric blender. Strain the clam liquor through a fine sieve lined with a double thickness of dampened cheesecloth and set over a bowl. Measure and reserve 2 cups of the liquor.

In a heavy 2- to 3-quart saucepan, melt the butter over moderate heat. When the foam begins to subside, add the flour and stir well. Then, stirring the mixture constantly with a wire whisk, pour in the clam liquor in a slow, thin stream and cook over high heat until the mixture comes to a boil, thickens lightly and is smooth. Reduce the heat to low, stir in the clams, thyme and pepper, and simmer partially covered for 15 minutes.

Stirring constantly, pour in the cream and simmer for a few minutes longer to heat the clam bisque through. Taste for seasoning, ladle the bisque into individual heated soup plates and serve at once.

Manhattan Clam Chowder

To serve 6

4 large firm ripe tomatoes, or
    substitute 4 cups chopped drained
    canned tomatoes
2 dozen large hard-shell clams *(see
    page 2),* shucked and drained,
    and their liquor
3 tablespoons butter
1 cup finely chopped onions

¼ cup finely chopped carrots
¼ cup finely chopped celery
3 cups water
1 medium-sized bay leaf
½ teaspoon crumbled dried thyme
Freshly ground black pepper
3 medium-sized boiling potatoes,
    peeled and cut into ¼-inch dice
    (about 2 cups)

If you are using fresh tomatoes, drop them into boiling water for 15 seconds, then peel off the skins with a small sharp knife. Cut out the stems and cut the tomatoes in half crosswise. Squeeze the halves to remove the juice and seeds, then coarsely chop the pulp. Canned tomatoes need only to be drained thoroughly and chopped.

Chop the clams fine and reserve them. Strain the clam liquor through a fine sieve lined with a double thickness of dampened cheesecloth; measure and save 3 cups of the liquor. (If there is less than 3 cups of liquor, add enough water to make that amount.)

In a heavy 3- to 4-quart saucepan, melt the butter over moderate heat. When the foam begins to subside, add the onions, carrots and celery and, stirring frequently, cook for about 5 minutes, or until the vegetables are soft but not brown. Add the chopped tomatoes, clam liquor, 3 cups of water, bay leaf, thyme and a few grindings of pepper, and bring to a boil over high heat. Reduce the heat to low, cover the pan partially and simmer for 45 minutes.

Stir in the potatoes and continue to simmer partially covered for about 12 minutes longer. Then add the chopped clams and cook the chowder for 2 to 3 minutes more. Pick out and discard the bay leaf.

Taste the chowder for seasoning and serve at once from a heated tureen or in individual soup plates.

Chicken-Corn Soup

To serve 8 to 12

2 pounds chicken backs and necks
10 cups water
2 medium-sized celery stalks
    including the green leaves, cut
    into 3-inch lengths
1 teaspoon whole black peppercorns
3 teaspoons salt
A 2½-pound chicken, cut into 6
    or 8 pieces
½ cup finely chopped celery
¼ cup finely chopped fresh parsley

Freshly ground black pepper
½ pound egg noodles, ¼ inch
    wide, preferably homemade
    (page 4), broken into
    3-inch pieces
2 cups fresh corn kernels, cut from
    about 4 large ears of corn, or
    substitute 2 cups thoroughly
    defrosted frozen corn
A pinch of crumbled saffron threads
    or ground saffron

Combine the chicken backs and necks and the water in a 6- to 8-quart casserole and bring to a boil over high heat, meanwhile skimming off the foam and scum as they rise to the surface. Add the cut-up celery, the peppercorns and 2 teaspoons of the salt, reduce the heat to low, and simmer partially covered for 45 minutes.

With a slotted spoon or kitchen tongs, remove and discard the chicken backs and necks and the celery. Add the cut-up chicken to the stock and bring to a boil over high heat, skimming the surface of foam and scum until it remains clear. Reduce the heat to low and simmer partially covered for about 30 minutes.

When the chicken is tender but still intact, transfer it to a plate. With a small sharp knife, remove the skin from the chicken and cut the meat from the bones. Discard the skin and bones; cut the chicken meat into ½-inch pieces and set aside.

Strain the stock through a fine sieve and return it to the pot. Add the finely chopped celery, the parsley, the remaining 1 teaspoon of salt and a few grindings of black pepper, and bring to a boil over high heat.

Stir in the noodles, corn and saffron, and cook uncovered over moderate heat for about 15 minutes, or until the noodles show only slight resistance to the bite. Add the reserved chicken and cook for a minute or so to heat it through.

Taste the chicken-corn soup for seasoning and serve at once from a heated tureen or in individual bowls.

Dried-Mushroom Soup

To serve 6 to 8

¼ pound dried wild mushrooms, or substitute ¼ pound imported European dried mushrooms, preferably the Polish variety
6 cups boiling water
4 to 5 cups chicken stock, fresh or canned

3 tablespoons butter
1½ cups finely chopped onions
½ cup cornstarch
Salt
Freshly ground black pepper
½ cup heavy cream, chilled

Place the dried mushrooms in a deep bowl, pour the boiling water over them, and soak for at least 2 hours, or until the mushrooms are soft and flexible. Drain the mushrooms through a fine sieve set over a bowl and reserve the soaking liquid. Rinse the mushrooms well under cold running water to remove any remaining traces of sand, cut them into thin slices, and drop them into a heavy 4- to 5-quart saucepan.

To clarify the soaking liquid, line the fine sieve with a double thickness of dampened cheesecloth. Pour in the liquid and strain it through the sieve directly into the saucepan. Stir in 3 cups of the chicken stock and bring to a boil over high heat. Reduce the heat to its lowest setting and simmer, partially covered, for 2 to 3 hours, or until the stock has the intensity of mushroom flavor you like.

In a heavy 8- to 10-inch skillet melt the butter over moderate heat. When the foam begins to subside, add the onions and, stirring frequently, cook for 8 to 10 minutes, or until they are golden brown. Watch carefully for any sign of burning and regulate the heat accordingly.

With a rubber spatula, scrape the contents of the skillet into the simmering soup. In a small bowl, stir the cornstarch and 1 cup of chicken stock together to make a smooth paste. Stirring the soup constantly with a large spoon, pour in the cornstarch mixture in a slow, thin stream and cook over moderate heat until the soup comes to a boil, thickens and is smooth. Taste and season with salt and a few grindings of black pepper. (If the soup is too thick for your taste, thin it with up to 1 cup of additional chicken stock.)

Just before serving, pour the cream into a chilled bowl. With a wire whisk or a rotary or electric beater, whip the cream until it is stiff enough to stand in firm peaks on the beater when it is lifted from the bowl.

Ladle the mushroom soup into individual heated soup plates and top each serving with a spoonful or so of whipped cream. Serve at once.

VEGETABLES & SALADS

Batter-fried Mushrooms

To serve 4 to 6 as a first course

1 cup unsifted flour	2 dozen firm fresh mushrooms, each
1 cup beer, at room temperature	about 2 inches in diameter
Vegetable oil for deep frying	Salt

Sift the flour into a deep bowl and make a well in the center. Slowly pour in the beer and, stirring gently, gradually incorporate the flour. Stir until the mixture is smooth, but do not beat or overmix. Set the batter aside uncovered to rest at room temperature for 3 hours before using.

Preheat the oven to its lowest setting. Meanwhile, line a large shallow baking dish or jelly-roll pan with a double thickness of paper towels and place it in the middle of the oven. Pour vegetable oil into a deep fryer or large heavy saucepan to a depth of about 3 inches and heat the oil until it reaches a temperature of 375° on a deep-frying thermometer.

Trim off the ends of the mushroom stems with a small sharp knife and wipe the caps and stems with a dampened kitchen towel. One at a time, pick up a mushroom with tongs or a slotted spoon, immerse it in the batter and, when it is well coated on all sides, drop it into the hot oil. Deep-fry 4 or 5 mushrooms at a time for about 4 minutes, turning them occasionally until they are delicately and evenly browned. As they are fried, transfer the mushrooms to the paper-lined pan and keep them warm in the oven while you coat and deep-fry the rest.

Arrange the mushrooms on a heated platter and sprinkle them lightly with salt just before serving.

Summer Squash Soufflé

To serve 4 to 6

5 or 6 medium-sized firm ripe
    yellow summer squash (about
2 pounds), peeled and cut into
    1-inch chunks
1 tablespoon butter, softened, plus
    4 tablespoons butter

1 cup finely chopped onions
2 egg yolks, lightly beaten
A pinch of ground nutmeg,
    preferably freshly grated
1 teaspoon salt
Freshly ground black pepper
2 egg whites

Pour water into the lower part of a steamer to within about 1 inch of the top pan. Bring the water to a boil, put the squash in the top pan and set it in place. Immediately cover the pan and steam over high heat for 15 to 20 minutes, or until the squash is tender.

(Lacking a steamer, you can improvise one by using a large pot equipped with a tightly fitting cover and a standing colander or a collapsible steaming basket on legs. Pour water into the pot to within 1 inch of the perforated container and bring it to a boil. Place the squash in the basket or colander, set it in place, and cover the pot. Steam over high heat for 15 to 20 minutes, or until the squash is soft.)

Purée the squash through a food mill or mash it to a smooth purée with a fork. Then transfer the purée to a fine sieve set over a deep mixing bowl and press the squash down with the back of a spoon to extract as much of the excess liquid as possible. Discard the liquid and transfer the squash to the bowl.

Preheat the oven to 350°. With a pastry brush, spread the tablespoon of softened butter evenly over the bottom and sides of a 1-quart casserole or soufflé dish. Set aside.

In a heavy 8- to 10-inch skillet, melt the remaining 4 tablespoons of butter over moderate heat. When the foam begins to subside, add the onions and, stirring frequently, cook for about 5 minutes, or until they are soft and translucent but not brown. Stir the onions into the puréed squash. Then beat in the egg yolks, nutmeg, salt and a few grindings of pepper.

With a wire whisk or a rotary or electric beater, beat the egg whites until they are stiff enough to stand in unwavering peaks on the beater when it is lifted from the bowl. With a rubber spatula, scoop the whites over the squash mixture and fold them together gently but thoroughly.

Pour the soufflé into the buttered dish, spreading it evenly and smoothing the top with the spatula. Bake in the middle of the oven for about 40 minutes, or until the soufflé puffs up above the rim of the dish and the top is lightly browned. Serve at once directly from the baking dish.

Fresh Asparagus with Lemon Cream Sauce, Shaker Style

To serve 4

2 pounds fresh asparagus
1¼ teaspoons salt
1 cup light cream
2 tablespoons butter
1 teaspoon finely cut fresh mint
1 egg yolk, lightly beaten
1 teaspoon strained fresh lemon
  juice
½ teaspoon ground nutmeg,
  preferably freshly grated

Line up the asparagus tips on a chopping board and cut off the ends so that the spears are the same length. With a small sharp knife, peel off the tough outer skin of each spear. At the end, the peel may be as thick as ⅛₆ inch but it will become paper-thin toward the tip. Divide the spears into four equal bundles and tie each bundle at both ends with string.

In a 4- to 5-quart enameled or stainless-steel casserole, bring 2 quarts of water and 1 teaspoon of the salt to a boil over high heat. Drop in the asparagus and cook briskly, uncovered, for 8 to 10 minutes, or until the stalks are barely tender and show slight resistance when pierced with the point of a small, sharp knife.

With two kitchen forks, lift the bundles out of the water by their strings. Cut off the strings, spread the asparagus on paper towels to drain, then transfer them to a heated platter. Drape loosely with foil to keep the asparagus warm while you prepare the sauce.

In a heavy 6- to 8-inch skillet, combine the cream, butter, mint and the remaining ¼ teaspoon of salt. Bring to a boil over high heat and, stirring frequently, boil for 5 minutes, or until the cream has reduced to about ¾ of a cup. Then reduce the heat to low. Add about 2 tablespoons of the cream to the egg yolk and mix well. Stirring constantly, gradually pour the mixture into the cream and simmer gently for a minute or so. Do not let the sauce come anywhere near a boil or it will curdle. Stir in the lemon juice, taste for seasoning, and pour the sauce over the asparagus. Sprinkle with nutmeg and serve at once.

Fresh Spinach and Herbs, Shaker Style

To serve 4

2 pounds fresh spinach
4 tablespoons butter
¼ cup finely cut scallions,
   including 2 inches of the green
   tops

½ teaspoon crumbled dried
   rosemary
1 tablespoon finely chopped fresh
   parsley
1 teaspoon salt
Freshly ground black pepper

With a small sharp knife, cut away the ends of the spinach, the tough stems and any bruised or yellow leaves. Pile the leaves in small stacks and chop them fine. Then wash the spinach in a sieve or colander set under cold running water.

Drop the spinach into a 4- to 5-quart enameled saucepan, cover tightly and cook over moderate heat for about 8 minutes. Drain the spinach in a colander and, a handful at a time, squeeze the leaves vigorously until they are completely dry. Set aside.

In a heavy 8- to 10-inch skillet, melt the butter over moderate heat. When the foam begins to subside, add the scallions and rosemary and, stirring frequently, cook for about 5 minutes, until the scallions are soft and translucent but not brown. Add the spinach, parsley, salt and pepper and stir over low heat for a minute or so to heat the spinach through. Taste for seasoning and serve at once.

Broccoli Purée

To serve 6 to 8

3 pounds firm fresh broccoli
8 tablespoons butter, cut into
   ½-inch bits and softened
¼ teaspoon ground nutmeg,

   preferably freshly grated
1 teaspoon salt
Freshly ground black pepper
1 hard-cooked egg, finely chopped

With a small sharp knife, cut the broccoli flowerets from their stalks. Trim off and discard the tough woody ends of the stalks, then peel each of them deeply enough with the knife to expose the pale green flesh. Slice the stalks into 2-inch lengths.

Drop the stalks and flowerets into enough lightly salted boiling water to cover them by at least 2 inches. Boil briskly, uncovered, for 8 to 10 minutes, or until a piece of the stalk can be easily mashed against the side of the pan with the back of a fork. Thoroughly drain the broccoli in a large sieve or colander, shaking it from side to side to remove any clinging water. Then purée the broccoli through the coarse blade of a food mill or rub it through a coarse sieve with the back of a spoon.

Return the purée to the saucepan and, stirring constantly, cook over low heat until almost all of its moisture has evaporated. Stir in the softened butter bits, the nutmeg, salt and a few grindings of pepper. Taste for seasoning. Mound the broccoli purée in a heated serving dish, garnish the top with the chopped egg and serve at once.

Corn Custard

To serve 4 to 6

2 cups fresh corn kernels, cut from
    about 4 large ears of corn, or
    substitute 2 cups frozen corn
    kernels, thoroughly defrosted
4 eggs
1 cup heavy cream
½ cup milk
¼ cup flour
1 tablespoon sugar
1 teaspoon salt
⅛ teaspoon ground white pepper

Preheat the oven to 350°. Place the corn in the jar of an electric blender and blend at high speed for 30 seconds. Turn off the machine, scrape down the sides of the jar with a rubber spatula, and blend the corn to a purée. Add the eggs, cream, milk, flour, sugar, salt and pepper, and continue to blend until the mixture is smooth and thick.

Pour the mixture into an ungreased 1½-quart soufflé dish and place the dish in a deep roasting pan set on the middle shelf of the oven. Then pour in enough boiling water to come about two thirds of the way up the sides of the dish. Bake for about 1 hour, or until the top is golden brown and a knife inserted in the center comes out clean. Serve at once.

Potato Filling

To serve 4 to 6

1 tablespoon butter, softened, plus
  9 tablespoons butter, cut into
  ¼-inch bits
3 medium-sized boiling potatoes,
  peeled and quartered
¼ cup milk
½ teaspoon salt

¼ teaspoon white pepper
½ cup finely chopped onions
4 to 5 slices homemade-type white
  bread, cut into ¼-inch cubes
  (about 2 cups)
2 eggs, lightly beaten
¼ cup finely chopped fresh parsley

Traditionally, Pennsylvania Dutch potato filling is served as a side dish, and is used only occasionally to stuff chickens or turkeys.

Preheat the oven to 350°. With a pastry brush, spread the tablespoon of softened butter evenly over the bottom and sides of a 1-quart baking-and-serving dish. Set aside.

Drop the potatoes into enough lightly salted boiling water to cover them completely. Boil briskly, uncovered, until a potato quarter is soft enough to be mashed easily against the side of the pan with a fork.

Drain the potatoes in a sieve or colander, and pat them dry with paper towels. Purée the potatoes through a food ricer into a bowl, or place them in the bowl and mash them with the back of a fork. Beat in the milk, salt and white pepper.

Meanwhile, melt 8 tablespoons of the butter bits in a heavy 8- to 10-inch skillet over moderate heat. When the foam begins to subside, add the onions and, stirring frequently, cook for about 5 minutes, or until they are soft and translucent but not brown. With a slotted spoon, add the onions to the potatoes.

Fry the bread cubes in the butter remaining in the skillet, stirring them frequently until they are crisp and lightly browned. Add the bread cubes, eggs and parsley to the potatoes. Beat vigorously with a wooden spoon for 2 or 3 minutes, then spoon the mixture into the baking dish and smooth the top with a rubber spatula. Sprinkle the remaining tablespoon of butter bits over the potato filling.

Bake in the middle of the oven for 35 minutes, or until the top is golden brown and crusty. Serve at once as an accompaniment to meat or fowl.

Sautéed Potato Balls

To serve 4 to 6

½ pound unsalted butter, cut into
   ½-inch bits
9 medium-sized boiling potatoes
   (about 3 pounds)

First clarify the butter in the following fashion: In a small heavy sauce-pan, melt the butter over low heat, turning the bits about with a spoon so that they melt slowly and completely without browning. Remove the pan from the heat and let the butter rest for a minute or so. Then skim off and discard the foam. Tipping the pan slightly, spoon the clear butter into a bowl. (There will be about 12 tablespoons.) Discard the milky solids left in the pan.

Peel the potatoes and, with a melon baller or small knife, cut them into balls about 1 inch in diameter. Spread the potato balls on paper towels, and pat them completely dry with fresh towels.

In a heavy 10- to 12-inch skillet, warm 8 tablespoons of the clarified butter over moderate heat. When the butter is hot, drop in the potatoes and brown them lightly. Slide the pan back and forth occasionally to roll the balls around and regulate the heat so that they color evenly without burning. Add more clarified butter by the tablespoonful if necessary.

Reduce the heat to low, cover the skillet tightly and cook for 12 to 15 minutes, still sliding the pan back and forth from time to time. The potatoes are done when they are golden brown and show no resistance when pierced deeply with the point of a small sharp knife. Serve at once.

Mushroom-stuffed Potatoes

To serve 6

3 tablespoons butter, softened
6 eight-ounce baking potatoes,
  thoroughly scrubbed and patted
  dry with paper towels
6 slices lean bacon
1 cup finely chopped fresh
  mushrooms
¾ cup light cream
2 egg yolks, lightly beaten
1 tablespoon finely chopped fresh
  chives
6 tablespoons freshly grated Swiss
  cheese

Preheat the oven to 425°. With a pastry brush, spread 2 tablespoons of the softened butter evenly over the skins of the potatoes. Arrange the potatoes side by side on a wire rack set in a jelly-roll pan and bake in the middle of the oven for about 1 hour. The potatoes are done if they feel soft when squeezed gently between your thumb and forefinger. Remove the potatoes and reduce the oven temperature to 375°.

Brush the remaining tablespoon of butter over the bottom of a shallow baking dish large enough to hold the potatoes in one layer. Set aside.

In a heavy 8- to 10-inch skillet, fry the bacon over moderate heat, turning the slices frequently with tongs until they are crisp and brown and have rendered all their fat. Transfer the bacon to paper towels to drain, and crumble it coarsely.

Pour off all but about 4 tablespoons of the fat remaining in the skillet. Add the mushrooms and, stirring from time to time, cook for 5 to 10 minutes but do not let them brown. When the moisture in the pan has evaporated, transfer the mushrooms to a bowl and set aside.

Cut a ¼-inch-thick slice lengthwise off the top of each baked potato. With a spoon, scoop out the potato pulp, leaving the skin intact and creating a boatlike shell about ¼ inch thick.

Purée the potato pulp through a ricer into a deep bowl, or place the pulp in a bowl and mash it to a smooth purée with the back of a table fork. Beat in the cream and egg yolks and, when they are completely incorporated, stir in the chives, the reserved bacon bits and the mushrooms. Taste for seasoning.

Spoon the potato mixture into the shells, mounding it in the center. Arrange the shells in the buttered dish and sprinkle the cheese on top. Bake in the middle of the oven until the potatoes are golden brown and crusty. Serve at once.

Cauliflower with Buttered Crumbs

To serve 6

A 1½- to 2-pound firm
   unblemished cauliflower
8 tablespoons butter, cut into
   ½-inch bits
½ cup soft fresh crumbs made
   from homemade-type white
   bread, pulverized in a blender or
   finely shredded with a fork

Cut away the thick stem at the base of the cauliflower and break off the green leaves. Wash the cauliflower thoroughly under cold running water. Then drop the cauliflower into enough lightly salted boiling water to cover it completely and boil uncovered for about 20 minutes, or until the core shows only the slightest resistance when pierced deeply with the point of a small sharp knife. Drain the cauliflower in a colander and place it on a heated platter.

In a heavy 6- to 8-inch skillet, melt the butter bits over moderate heat. When the foam begins to subside add the crumbs and, stirring frequently, fry them until they are crisp and golden brown. Dribble the crumbs and butter over the cauliflower and serve at once.

Shaker Salad

To serve 4 to 6

½ pound green string beans, trimmed, washed and cut into 1½-inch lengths
3 tablespoons tarragon vinegar
1 tablespoon finely chopped onions
½ teaspoon crumbled dried thyme
½ teaspoon crumbled dried savory
½ teaspoon dry mustard
1 teaspoon salt
Freshly ground black pepper
½ cup olive or vegetable oil or a combination of both
2 firm heads bibb or Boston lettuce, trimmed, washed, separated in leaves and cut into 1-inch pieces (about 3 cups)
2 tablespoons finely chopped scallions, including 1 inch of the green tops

Drop the string beans into enough lightly salted boiling water to cover them by at least 1 inch. Boil briskly, uncovered, for 4 to 5 minutes, or until the beans are tender but still somewhat crisp to the bite. Drain the beans in a sieve or colander and run cold water over them to cool them quickly and set their color. Spread the beans on paper towels to drain and pat them dry with fresh paper towels. Refrigerate until ready to serve.

Just before serving, combine the vinegar, onions, thyme, savory, dry mustard, salt and a few grindings of pepper in a serving bowl and mix well with a wire whisk. Whisking constantly, pour in the oil in a slow stream and stir until the dressing is smooth and thick. Add the beans, lettuce and scallions, and toss together gently but thoroughly. Serve at once.

Celery Slaw

To serve 4 to 6

1 medium-sized bunch of celery (about 1 pound)
¼ cup wine vinegar
1 tablespoon sugar
¼ teaspoon paprika
2 teaspoons salt
Freshly ground black pepper
⅔ cup vegetable oil
½ cup sour cream
1 medium-sized onion, peeled, cut crosswise into ⅛-inch-thick slices and separated into rings
1 pimiento, cut into strips about 1 inch long and ⅛ inch wide

With a small sharp knife, remove the leaves from the celery. Separate the celery into individual ribs, trim the roots ends with the knife and scrape off the heavy outside strings and any brown blemished areas. Wash the ribs thoroughly under cold running water and pat them dry with paper towels. Then, holding the knife at a diagonal, cut the ribs crosswise into ⅛-inch-thick slices, and drop them into a large bowl. Set aside.

Combine the vinegar, sugar, paprika, salt and a few grindings of pepper in a small deep bowl and beat with a wire whisk until the sugar dissolves. Whisking the mixture constantly, pour in the vegetable oil in a very slow, thin stream. When the sauce thickens and is smooth, beat in the sour cream with the whisk. Taste for seasoning.

Pour the sauce over the celery, add the onion rings and toss together gently but thoroughly. Cover with foil or plastic wrap and marinate in the refrigerator for about 3 hours.

Just before serving, taste for seasoning again and gently stir in the pimiento strips.

Waldorf Salad

To serve 6 to 8

3 large firm ripe apples, cored and cut into ½-inch pieces (about 4 cups)
2 tablespoons strained fresh lemon juice
3 medium-sized celery stalks, trimmed and cut into ¼-inch dice (about 2 cups)

1 cup coarsely chopped walnuts
1 cup freshly made mayonnaise (page 7), or substitute unsweetened bottled mayonnaise
½ cup heavy cream
1 or 2 heads Boston or bibb lettuce, separated into leaves, washed, patted dry and chilled

Oscar Tschirky, who was known as Oscar of the Waldorf and was the maître d'hôtel of the famous Manhattan establishment from 1893 to 1943, invented Waldorf salad. The original version was composed of apples, celery and mayonnaise, served on lettuce. Though chopped walnuts were added later, they have become an almost indispensable ingredient.

Combine the apples and lemon juice in a deep bowl and turn the apple pieces about gently with a spoon to moisten them evenly. Stir in the celery and walnuts. Then, in another bowl, mix the mayonnaise and cream and, when the mixture is smooth, pour it over the apples. Toss all the ingredients together gently but thoroughly.

Shape the lettuce leaves into cups on 6 or 8 chilled individual serving plates. Mound the Waldorf salad in the cups, dividing it evenly among them. Serve at once.

MEAT

Braised Pork Chops

To serve 6

6 eight-ounce loin pork chops, cut about 1 inch thick
1 tablespoon salt
Freshly ground black pepper
¼ cup vegetable oil

1 cup finely chopped onions
1 teaspoon finely chopped garlic
2 cups water
2 tablespoons distilled white vinegar

Pat the pork chops completely dry with paper towels and season them on both sides with the salt and a liberal grinding of pepper.

In a heavy 12-inch skillet, heat the oil over moderate heat until a light haze forms above it. Add the pork chops and, turning them occasionally with a spatula, fry the chops for about 15 minutes, or until they are richly and evenly browned. Stir in the onions and garlic, add the water and bring to a boil over high heat. Reduce the heat to low, cover tightly and simmer for about 30 minutes, turning the chops over 2 or 3 times.

Arrange the pork chops attractively on a heated platter. Then stir the vinegar into the cooking liquid, taste for seasoning and pour the sauce over the chops. Serve at once.

Pot-roasted Loin of Pork

To serve 6 to 8

A 5-pound pork loin in one piece,
  with the excess fat removed,
  finely chopped and reserved, and
  with the backbone (chine) sawed
  through at ½-inch intervals, but
  left attached and tied to the loin
  in 2 or 3 places
3 tablespoons flour
2 large onions, peeled and cut
  crosswise into ¼-inch-thick slices

1 teaspoon finely chopped garlic
3 medium-sized carrots, scraped and
  finely chopped
1 cup dry white wine
½ cup chicken stock, fresh or
  canned
½ teaspoon crumbled dried thyme
½ teaspoon paprika
2 teaspoons salt
Freshly ground black pepper

Preheat the oven to 350°. Pat the pork loin completely dry with paper towels, then sprinkle it on all sides with the flour and spread the flour evenly with your fingers.

In a heavy 6- to 8-quart casserole, fry the reserved pork fat over moderate heat, turning the bits about frequently with a slotted spoon until they are crisp and have rendered all their fat. Remove and discard the bits. Brown the pork loin in the fat, turning it over frequently and regulating the heat so that it colors richly and evenly without burning.

Transfer the pork loin to a plate and add the onions and garlic to the fat remaining in the casserole. Stirring frequently, cook over moderate heat for about 5 minutes, or until the onions are soft and translucent but not brown. Add the carrots and cook for a minute or so longer.

Stir in the wine, chicken stock, thyme, paprika, salt and a few grindings of pepper, and bring to a boil over high heat, meanwhile scraping in any brown particles that cling to the bottom and sides of the casserole. Return the pork loin and the liquid that has accumulated around it and cover the casserole tightly. Braise in the middle of the oven for about 1½ hours, or until the pork shows no resistance when pierced deeply with the point of a small skewer or sharp knife.

Place the pork loin on a heated platter. With a slotted spoon, skim as much fat as possible from the surface of the cooking liquid. Then strain the liquid through a fine sieve into a bowl, pressing down hard on the vegetables with the back of a spoon to extract all their juices before discarding the pulp. Moisten the pork with a little of the gravy, pour the rest into a sauceboat and serve at once.

Pasties, Michigan Style

To make six 9-inch pasties

4 cups unsifted flour
2 teaspoons ~~plus 1 tablespoon~~ salt
1½ cups lard (¾ pound), chilled
    and cut into ¼-inch bits
10 to 12 tablespoons ice water
2 pounds top round steak, trimmed
    of fat and cut into ¼-inch cubes
5 medium-sized boiling potatoes

(about 1½ pounds), peeled and
    coarsely chopped
3 medium-sized turnips, scraped
    and cut into ¼-inch cubes
    (about 1½ cups)
1½ cups finely chopped onions
1 teaspoon freshly ground black
    pepper + salt

In a large chilled bowl combine the flour, 2 teaspoons of the salt and the lard. Working quickly, rub the flour and fat together with your fingertips until it looks like flakes of coarse meal. Pour in 10 tablespoons of ice water, toss together, and gather the dough into a ball. If the dough crumbles, add up to 2 tablespoons more water, a teaspoonful at a time, until the particles adhere. Divide the dough into 6 equal balls, dust them with flour and wrap in wax paper. Refrigerate for at least 1 hour.

Preheat the oven to 400°. Combine the beef, potatoes, turnips, onions, the tablespoon of salt and the pepper in a bowl and stir them together.

On a lightly floured surface, roll out one ball of dough at a time into a rough circle about ¼ inch thick. Using a plate or pot lid about 9 inches in diameter as a guide, cut the dough into a round with a pastry wheel or sharp knife. Place about 1½ cups of the filling mixture on the round, and fold and shape the pasty as shown below. With a large spatula, carefully transfer the pasty to an ungreased baking sheet. Then repeat the procedure to roll, fill and shape the remaining pasties.

Bake in the middle of the oven for 45 minutes, or until the pasties are golden brown. Serve them hot, or at room temperature.

PUTTING A PASTY TOGETHER
Roll out all of the pasty dough and cut it into 9-inch rounds. For each pasty, spread 1½ cups of the filling in a strip across the center of the round *(left)*. Fold one side of the round up over the filling. Then turn up the other side of the round and press the edges of the dough together snugly at one end *(below)*.

Smoked Pork Chops and Lentils

To serve 6

¼ cup vegetable oil
1 teaspoon finely chopped garlic
2½ cups chicken stock, fresh or
    canned
2½ cups dried lentils
1 cup finely chopped scallions,
    including 2 inches of the green
    tops
¼ cup finely chopped fresh parsley
6 six-ounce smoked loin pork chops,
    each cut about 1 inch thick

In a heavy 4- to 5-quart casserole, heat the vegetable oil over moderate heat until a light haze forms above it. Add the garlic and stir for a minute or so, then pour in the chicken stock and bring to a boil over high heat. Stir in the lentils, scallions and parsley and, when the mixture returns to a boil, add the pork chops and turn them about with kitchen tongs to moisten them evenly.

Cover the casserole tightly, reduce the heat to low and simmer for about 45 minutes, or until the lentils are tender but not falling apart. Taste for seasoning and serve at once, directly from the casserole or, if you prefer, mound the lentils on a heated platter and arrange the pork chops attractively around them.

Starting from the sealed end, press the two edges of the round together to encase the filling securely and form a double-thick band of dough about ½ inch wide along the seam *(below)*. With your fingers, crimp the band into a decorative rope or scalloped fluting. When it is ready for baking, the shaped pasty should resemble the ones shown at right.

Flank Steak with Meat Stuffing, Shaker Style

To serve 6 to 8

A 2- to 2½-pound flank steak,
  thoroughly trimmed
8 tablespoons butter
4 or 5 slices homemade-type white
  bread, cut into ¼-inch cubes
  (2 cups)
1 cup finely chopped onions
1 cup finely chopped celery
¼ pound lean ground beef
¼ pound lean ground veal
¼ pound lean ground pork
1 egg
¼ cup finely chopped fresh parsley
¼ teaspoon crumbled dried
  rosemary
½ teaspoon crumbled dried basil
½ teaspoon crumbled dried savory

¼ teaspoon ground sage
1½ teaspoons salt
¼ teaspoon freshly ground black
  pepper
2 tablespoons vegetable oil
2 medium-sized celery stalks,
  trimmed, leaves removed, cut
  crosswise into ¼-inch-thick
  slices
1 medium-sized onion, peeled and
  cut crosswise into ¼-inch-thick
  slices
1 medium-sized carrot, scraped and
  coarsely chopped
1 cup beef stock, fresh or canned,
  or 1 cup water or a combination
  of the two

Ask your butcher to cut a pocket in the steak, or do it yourself in the following manner: With a long, very sharp knife, slit the steak horizontally from one of the long sides, cutting through the steak to within about ½ inch of the other long side and to within about 1 inch of each short end.

Preheat the oven to 350°. In a heavy 8- to 10-inch skillet, melt 4 tablespoons of the butter over moderate heat. Add the bread cubes and, stirring frequently, fry them until they are crisp and golden brown. With a slotted spoon, transfer the cubes to a deep bowl.

Melt 2 more tablespoons of butter in the skillet, add the chopped onions and chopped celery and stir for about 5 minutes, until they are soft but not brown. With a rubber spatula, scrape the onions and celery over the bread cubes. Add the ground beef, veal, pork, egg, parsley, rosemary, basil, savory, sage, salt and pepper. Knead vigorously with both hands, then beat with a wooden spoon until all the ingredients are well blended.

Holding the steak upright on its long closed side, pack the stuffing tightly into the pocket, a handful at a time. Then lay the steak flat and close the open side by sewing it with a large needle and white thread.

Melt the remaining 2 tablespoons of butter with the oil in a heavy casserole large enough to hold the steak comfortably. Brown the steak in the hot fat, turning it with two spoons and regulating the heat so that the meat colors richly and evenly on both sides without burning. Transfer the steak to a plate and add the sliced celery, sliced onion and carrot to the fat remaining in the casserole. Stirring frequently, cook for 8 to 10 minutes, or until the vegetables are soft and delicately browned.

Pour in the stock or water or stock-and-water combination and bring to a boil over high heat, meanwhile scraping in the brown particles clinging to the bottom and sides of the pan. Return the steak to the casserole together with any juices that have accumulated around it. Cover tightly and braise in the middle of the oven for 1 hour, or until the steak shows no resistance when pierced deeply with the point of a small sharp knife. Place the steak on a heated platter. Remove the thread.

Skim off the surface fat and strain the cooking liquid through a fine sieve into a sauceboat or bowl, pressing down hard on the vegetables with the back of a spoon to extract all their juices before discarding the pulp. Taste for seasoning, and serve the gravy separately with the steak.

Deviled Short Ribs

To serve 4

¼ cup finely chopped onions
¼ cup strained fresh lemon juice
¼ cup vegetable oil
3 tablespoons prepared mustard
1 teaspoon finely chopped garlic
2 teaspoons salt
Freshly ground black pepper
3 pounds lean short ribs of beef,
    each 4 to 5 inches long

Combine the onions, lemon juice, oil, mustard, garlic, salt and a liberal grinding of pepper in a deep bowl and mix them well. Add the short ribs and turn them about with a spoon until they are evenly coated. Then let the ribs marinate at room temperature for about 2 hours, turning them from time to time.

Preheat the oven to 400°. Arrange the ribs fat side up in a single layer on a rack set in a shallow roasting pan. (Discard the remaining marinade.) Roast the ribs uncovered in the middle of the oven for 20 minutes. Then reduce the heat to 350° and continue to roast for 1 hour and 15 minutes longer, or until the meat is tender and shows no resistance when pierced with the point of a small skewer or sharp knife. Arrange the ribs attractively on a heated platter and serve at once.

Beef Potpie

To serve 4 to 6

BEEF

2 pounds lean beef chuck, trimmed
   of excess fat and cut into 1-inch
   cubes
2 teaspoons salt
¼ teaspoon freshly ground black
   pepper
½ cup flour
¼ cup vegetable oil
½ cup finely chopped onions

1 teaspoon finely chopped garlic
1 quart water
1 medium-sized bay leaf
3 medium-sized boiling potatoes,
   peeled and cut into 1-inch cubes
   (about 3 cups)
4 medium-sized carrots, scraped and
   cut crosswise into ¼-inch-thick
   rounds
¼ cup finely chopped fresh parsley

Pat the cubes of beef completely dry with paper towels and sprinkle them on all sides with the salt and pepper. Dip them in the flour to coat them lightly and shake off the excess flour.

In a heavy 3- to 4-quart casserole, heat the oil over moderate heat until a light haze forms above it. Brown the beef cubes in the oil, 4 or 5 at a time, turning them about with a slotted spatula and regulating the heat so that they color richly and evenly without burning. As they brown, transfer the beef cubes to a plate.

Add the onions and garlic to the fat remaining in the casserole and, stirring frequently, cook for about 5 minutes, until they are soft and translucent but not brown. Pour in the water and bring to a boil over high heat, meanwhile scraping in the brown particles clinging to the bottom and sides of the pan. Return the beef and the liquid that has accumulated around it to the pan, add the bay leaf, and reduce the heat to low.

Simmer partially covered for 1 hour, then add the potatoes, carrots and parsley. Partially cover the pan again and simmer for 20 to 30 minutes longer, or until the vegetables are tender but still intact. (As the beef and vegetables simmer, check the casserole from time to time. If the liquid seems to be cooking away too rapidly, reduce the heat and add a little more water.) Remove the casserole from the heat, uncover the beef mixture and set aside to cool to room temperature.

TOPPING

Nonsweet short-crust pastry for a
   piecrust top *(page 6)*

1 egg lightly beaten with
   1 tablespoon milk

Meanwhile, preheat the oven to 375°. On a lightly floured surface, pat the pastry dough into a rough circle about 1 inch thick. Dust a little flour over and under it and roll it out from the center to within an inch of the far edge. Lift the dough and turn it 2 inches; then roll again from the center to within an inch or so of the far edge. Repeat—lifting, turning, rolling—until the circle is 12 inches in diameter and about ⅛ inch thick.

When the meat mixture has completely cooled, drape the dough over the rolling pin, lift it up and unroll it carefully over the casserole. Trim off the excess dough with scissors or a small knife, leaving a 1-inch over-hang all around the rim. Fold the overhang underneath the edges of the pastry and secure the dough to the rim by crimping it tightly with your fingers or the tines of a fork.

Cut three 2-inch-long diagonal slashes, spaced about 1 inch apart, in the top of the pie and brush the surface with the egg-and-milk mixture. Bake the pie in the middle of the oven for 45 to 50 minutes, or until the crust is golden brown. Serve at once directly from the baking dish.

Pigs' Feet Souse

To serve 4 to 6

6 pounds fresh pigs' feet (8 to 12, depending on size)	1 teaspoon freshly ground black pepper
1 cup finely chopped onions	3 quarts water
1 medium-sized bay leaf, crumbled	2½ cups distilled white vinegar
1 tablespoon salt	12 whole black peppercorns

Combine the pigs' feet, onions, bay leaf, salt, ground pepper and water in a heavy 8- to 10-quart casserole and bring to a boil over high heat. Reduce the heat to low, cover tightly and simmer for 1½ to 2 hours, or until the pigs' feet show no resistance when pierced deeply with the point of a skewer or small sharp knife.

With tongs, transfer the pigs' feet to a deep bowl. Strain the cooking liquid through a fine sieve set over another bowl, pressing down hard on the onions with the back of a spoon to extract all their juices before discarding the pulp. Stir the vinegar and peppercorns into the strained liquid and pour the mixture over the pigs' feet. Cool to room temperature, then cover tightly with foil or plastic wrap and marinate in the refrigerator for at least 4 hours before serving. As it chills, the liquid will become a firm jelly. Serve the pigs' feet cold.

Martha Washington's Grand Leg of Lamb

To serve 8

2 pairs calf's sweetbreads (about 1½ pounds)

A 7-pound leg of lamb, boned but not split, with shank meat cut off

1½ teaspoons salt

Freshly ground black pepper

4 tablespoons butter, melted, plus 4 tablespoons butter, cut into ½-inch bits, plus 4 tablespoons butter, softened

1 tablespoon anchovy paste

4 tablespoons finely chopped fresh parsley

2 teaspoons capers, finely chopped

½ teaspoon crumbled dried thyme

¼ teaspoon finely grated fresh lemon peel

¼ teaspoon crumbled dried marjoram

1 cup soft fresh crumbs made from homemade-type white bread, pulverized in a blender or finely shredded with a fork

1 cup finely chopped onions

½ cup dry white wine

1½ to 2½ cups chicken stock, fresh or canned

12 breakfast-type pork sausages (about 1 pound)

¼ cup water

2 lamb kidneys, peeled and trimmed of fat

2 tablespoons strained fresh lemon juice

The yolks of 4 hard-cooked eggs

⅛ teaspoon ground white pepper

8 thin slices homemade-type white bread, cut into 3-inch rounds and fried in 4 tablespoons of butter

8 capers

16 flat anchovy fillets

Starting 6 hours or more ahead, soak the sweetbreads in several changes of cold water for 3 hours. Place them in a 4-quart enameled or stainless-steel pan and pour in 2 quarts of fresh cold water. Bring to a simmer slowly over moderate heat and blanch the sweetbreads by simmering them for 3 minutes. With tongs or a slotted spoon, transfer the sweetbreads to a bowl of cold water to rest for 1 or 2 minutes. Pat them dry with paper towels, and gently pull off as much of the outside membrane as possible.

Cut the two lobes from the tube between each pair of sweetbreads with a small sharp knife. Discard the tubes. Put the sweetbreads on a large flat platter. Cover them with a towel and weight them with a casserole or skillet weighing about 5 pounds to flatten and remove excess moisture from the sweetbreads. Refrigerate the sweetbreads for at least 2 hours.

Preheat the oven to 450°. Season the lamb on all sides with ½ teaspoon of salt and a few grindings of pepper. To prepare the stuffing, combine the 4 tablespoons of melted butter and 1 tablespoon of anchovy paste in a bowl and mix well. Add 2 tablespoons of parsley, the chopped capers, thyme, lemon peel and marjoram. Then stir in the bread crumbs.

Close the opening at the shank end of the leg of lamb by sewing it with a large needle and heavy white thread. Then fill the pocket in the lamb with the stuffing, and sew up the opening securely. Tie the leg of lamb crosswise in 5 or 6 places and lengthwise 2 or 3 times to hold it in a neat cylindrical shape. For the most predictable results, insert the tip of a meat thermometer at least 2 inches into the roast.

Set the lamb on a rack in a shallow roasting pan and roast it in the middle of the oven for 20 minutes. Reduce the oven temperature to 350°. Sprinkle the chopped onions around the lamb, roast 15 minutes more, and pour the wine and 1½ cups of chicken stock over the onions. Continue roasting for about 1 hour longer, or until the lamb is cooked to your taste. A meat thermometer will register 130° to 140° when the lamb is rare, 140° to 150° when medium, and 150° to 160° when well done. Ideally the lamb should be medium rare.

Half an hour or so before the lamb is ready to be served, prepare the garnishes: Combine the pork sausages and ¼ cup of water in a heavy 10- to 12-inch skillet and bring to a boil over high heat. Reduce the heat to low, cover tightly and simmer for 5 minutes. Then uncover the pan and, turning the sausages occasionally with a spatula, cook over moderate heat for about 5 minutes to brown them on all sides. Drain the sausages on paper towels, transfer them to a heated plate and cover with foil.

With a sharp knife, cut the sweetbreads crosswise into ½-inch-thick slices. Cut the kidneys crosswise into ¼-inch-thick slices and then cut the slices into ¼-inch-wide strips. In a heavy 10- to 12-inch skillet, melt 4 tablespoons of butter bits over moderate heat. When the foam begins to subside, add the sweetbreads and kidneys and, stirring frequently, fry for 6 to 8 minutes, or until the pieces are lightly browned. Add 2 tablespoons of lemon juice, ½ teaspoon of the salt and a few grindings of black pepper, and taste for seasoning. Remove the skillet from the heat and cover to keep the sweetbreads and kidneys warm.

Force the hard-cooked egg yolks through a fine sieve with the back of a spoon, then beat in the 4 tablespoons of softened butter. Add the remaining ½ teaspoon of salt and ⅛ teaspoon of white pepper, and taste for seasoning. Spoon the mixture into a pastry bag fitted with a star tube and pipe an egg-yolk rosette onto the center of each bread round. Set a caper on each rosette and arrange 2 anchovy fillets around it. Set aside.

When the leg of lamb has roasted its allotted time, transfer it to a large heated platter, and let it rest while you prepare the anchovy sauce.

ANCHOVY SAUCE
2 egg yolks
2 tablespoons flour

1 tablespoon anchovy paste
2 to 3 teaspoons strained fresh
    lemon juice

Strain the contents of the roasting pan through a fine sieve set over a 1-quart measuring cup, pressing down hard on the onions with the back of a spoon to extract all their juices. Pour the liquid into a small saucepan and add enough chicken stock to make 2 cups in all. Bring to a simmer

Continued on next page

over low heat. In a small bowl, beat the egg yolks, flour and 1 tablespoon of anchovy paste with a wire whisk until smooth. Ladle 2 or 3 tablespoons of simmering stock into the egg yolks and mix well. Whisking constantly, pour the yolks into the pan and cook over low heat until the sauce thickens lightly. Do not let the sauce come near a boil or the yolks will curdle. Taste and add 2 to 3 teaspoons of lemon juice.

To serve, mound the sweetbreads and kidneys at both the ends and sides of the leg of lamb and sprinkle them with the remaining 2 tablespoons of parsley. Arrange the sausages and bread rounds attractively on the platter, and present the anchovy sauce in a bowl or sauceboat.

Barbecued Venison Chops

To serve 6

¼ cup vegetable oil
6 six-ounce venison loin chops, cut about 1 inch thick
½ cup finely chopped onions
1 teaspoon finely chopped garlic
3 medium-sized firm ripe tomatoes, coarsely chopped and puréed

through a food mill or rubbed through a fine sieve with the back of a spoon
¼ cup strained fresh lemon juice
¼ cup Worcestershire sauce
1 teaspoon crumbled dried basil
1 teaspoon salt
Freshly ground black pepper

Preheat the oven to 400°. In a heavy 10- to 12-inch skillet, heat the oil over moderate heat until a light haze forms above it. Pat the venison chops completely dry with paper towels. Then brown them in the oil, 2 or 3 at a time, turning the chops frequently with tongs and regulating the heat so that they color richly and evenly without burning. As they brown, arrange the chops side by side in a shallow baking-serving dish large enough to hold them in one layer.

To prepare the barbecue sauce, add the onions and garlic to the fat remaining in the skillet. Stirring frequently, cook over moderate heat for about 5 minutes, until the onions are soft and translucent but not brown. Stir in the puréed tomatoes, lemon juice, Worcestershire, basil, salt and a few grindings of pepper.

Bring the sauce to a boil over high heat, stirring constantly and scraping in any brown particles clinging to the bottom and sides of the skillet. Taste for seasoning and pour the sauce evenly over the chops.

Bake uncovered in the middle of the oven for about 20 minutes, or until the chops show no resistance when pierced deeply with the point of a small sharp knife. Serve at once, directly from the baking dish.

Venison Stew

To serve 4 to 6

¼ pound salt pork, trimmed of all rind and cut into ¼-inch dice
2 pounds boneless venison, preferably loin, trimmed of all fat and cut into 2-inch cubes
½ cup flour
1 cup finely chopped onions
½ teaspoon finely chopped garlic
2 cups chicken stock, fresh or canned

1 medium-sized bay leaf, crumbled
½ teaspoon crumbled dried thyme
1 teaspoon salt
¼ teaspoon freshly ground black pepper
4 medium-sized boiling potatoes, peeled and quartered
2 medium-sized carrots, scraped and cut into 2-inch lengths
2 tablespoons distilled white vinegar

In a heavy 4- to 5-quart casserole, fry the salt pork over moderate heat, stirring the dice about with a slotted spoon until they are crisp and brown and have rendered all their fat. Transfer them to paper towels to drain, and pour off all but about 4 tablespoons of the fat from the pan.

Roll the cubes of venison in the flour to coat them evenly, then shake off the excess flour. Over high heat brown the venison in the fat remaining in the casserole, 4 or 5 pieces at a time. Turn the venison cubes about occasionally and regulate the heat so that they color richly and evenly without burning. As they brown, transfer the cubes to a plate.

When all the venison has been browned, add the onions and garlic to the casserole. Stirring occasionally, cook for 5 minutes, or until they are soft and translucent but not brown. Pour in the stock and bring to a boil over high heat. Add the bay leaf, thyme, salt and pepper and return the venison to the casserole together with the liquid that has accumulated around it. Reduce the heat to low, cover tightly and simmer for 1 hour.

Drop the potatoes and carrots into the casserole and turn them with a spoon to moisten them evenly. Continue to simmer covered for 20 to 30 minutes longer, or until the vegetables are tender and the venison shows no resistance when pierced deeply with the point of a small sharp knife. Stir in the vinegar and taste for seasoning. Then sprinkle the reserved pork bits on top and serve at once, directly from the casserole.

Sweetbreads en Coquille

To serve 4

2 pairs calf's sweetbreads (about
 1½ pounds)
1 tablespoon strained fresh lemon
 juice
3 teaspoons salt
1 tablespoon butter, softened, plus
 9 tablespoons butter, cut into
 ½-inch bits

1 cup finely chopped fresh
 mushrooms
6 tablespoons flour
2 cups light cream
⅛ teaspoon ground hot red pepper
 (cayenne)
¼ cup freshly grated imported
 Parmesan cheese

Soak the sweetbreads in several changes of cold water for 3 hours. Gently pull off as much of the outside membrane as possible without tearing the sweetbreads. Cut the two lobes of each pair from the tube between them with a small sharp knife. Discard both tubes.

Place the sweetbreads in an enameled saucepan with enough water to cover them by 2 inches, add the lemon juice and 2 teaspoons of the salt, and bring to a boil over high heat. Reduce the heat to its lowest point and simmer uncovered for about 15 minutes, or until the sweetbreads feel firm to the touch. Place the sweetbreads on paper towels to drain and pat them completely dry with fresh towels. Then cut them into ½-inch dice and set them aside on a plate.

Preheat the oven to 375°. With a pastry brush, spread the tablespoon of softened butter evenly over the bottoms and sides of four large scallop shells or four shallow individual baking dishes.

In a heavy 8- to 10-inch skillet, melt 3 tablespoons of the butter bits over moderate heat. When the foam begins to subside, add the mushrooms and, stirring occasionally, cook uncovered for 5 to 10 minutes but do not let them brown. When the moisture in the pan has evaporated completely, transfer the mushrooms to a bowl with a slotted spoon.

Add the remaining 6 tablespoons of butter bits to the skillet and melt over moderate heat. Then add the flour and mix well. Stirring the mixture constantly with a wire whisk, pour in the cream in a slow, thin stream and cook over high heat until the sauce comes to a boil, thickens heavily and is smooth. Reduce the heat to low and simmer for 2 to 3 minutes to remove any taste of raw flour.

Stir in the reserved sweetbreads and mushrooms, the remaining teaspoon of salt and the red pepper. Taste for seasoning and spoon the mixture into the buttered shells or baking dishes, dividing it evenly among them. Sprinkle the tops with the grated cheese.

Arrange the shells or dishes on a jelly-roll pan and bake in the upper third of the oven for 15 to 20 minutes, or until the sauce has begun to bubble and the top is lightly browned. If you like, slide the pan under a hot broiler for 30 seconds or so to brown the tops further. Serve at once.

Indiana Farm Sausage

To make 2 pounds

2 pounds lean ground pork
⅓ cup finely chopped onions
2 tablespoons crumbled dried sage
  leaves
1 tablespoon finely chopped fresh
  parsley
1 teaspoon crumbled dried thyme
1 teaspoon crumbled dried basil
1 teaspoon ground marjoram

1 teaspoon chili powder
1 teaspoon dried sweet pepper flakes
1 teaspoon ground hot red pepper
  (cayenne)
½ teaspoon finely chopped garlic
2 teaspoons salt
1 teaspoon freshly ground black
  pepper
2 tablespoons butter
2 tablespoons vegetable oil

In a deep bowl, combine the pork, onions, sage, parsley, thyme, basil, marjoram, chili powder, pepper flakes and ground red pepper, garlic, salt and black pepper. Knead vigorously with both hands, then beat with a wooden spoon until the mixture is light and fluffy.

Divide the mixture into halves and, on wax paper, shape and roll each half into a cylinder about 6 inches long and 2 inches in diameter. Wrap the sausages in fresh wax paper and refrigerate for at least 2 hours, or until firm to the touch.

Just before cooking, slice the sausages into rounds about ½ inch thick. In a heavy 10- to 12-inch skillet, melt the butter with the oil over moderate heat. When the foam begins to subside, add 5 or 6 sausage rounds and fry them for 3 or 4 minutes on each side. To test for doneness, pierce the sausages with the point of a knife. The juice that trickles out should be clear yellow; if it is tinged with pink, fry the sausages for a minute or so longer. Drain briefly on paper towels, then arrange the sausages on a heated platter and drape with foil to keep them warm while you fry the rest. Serve at once.

Schnitz und Kneppe

To serve 6

2 cups dried apples (½ pound)
3 pounds smoked ham butt

6 cups chicken stock, fresh or
  canned
2 tablespoons dark brown sugar

Place the dried apples in a small bowl and pour in enough water to cover them by at least 1 inch. Set the apples aside at room temperature to soak for at least 8 hours, or overnight. Drain the apples in a sieve or colander and discard the soaking water.

Place the ham butt in a heavy 5- to 6-quart casserole at least 12 inches in diameter and pour in enough water to cover the ham by 2 inches. Bring to a boil over high heat, reduce the heat to low, and simmer partially covered for 1½ hours, or until the ham shows no resistance when pierced deeply with the point of a small skewer or sharp knife. Transfer the ham to a plate and discard the cooking liquid.

With a sharp knife, cut the ham into ¼-inch-thick slices and then into ¼-inch cubes. Return the ham to the casserole and add the apples, chicken stock and brown sugar.

Bring to a boil over high heat, stirring until the sugar dissolves. Reduce the heat to low and simmer partially covered for 15 minutes. Taste for seasoning.

DUMPLINGS
2 cups unsifted flour
1 tablespoon double-acting
  baking powder

¼ teaspoon salt
2 tablespoons butter, cut into
  ¼-inch bits and softened
1½ cups milk

While the stew is simmering, prepare the dumpling dough: Combine the flour, baking powder and salt, and sift them into a deep bowl. Add the butter bits and, with your fingers, rub the flour and fat together until they look like flakes of coarse meal. Add the milk and beat vigorously with a spoon until the dough is smooth.

Drop the dumplings on top of the simmering stew by the heaping tablespoon. Cover the casserole tightly, and simmer undisturbed for about 10 minutes longer. The dumplings are done when they are puffed and fluffy and a cake tester or toothpick inserted in the center of a dumpling comes out clean.

Remove the dumplings with a slotted spoon and pour the ham-and-apple mixture into a preheated bowl or deep platter. Arrange the dumplings on top and serve at once.

Creamed Chipped Beef in Toasted Bread Cups

To serve 4

TOASTED BREAD CUPS
½ pound butter, melted
8 slices thinly sliced fresh
   homemade-type white bread,
   trimmed of crusts

Preheat the oven to 375°. With a pastry brush, spread the melted butter liberally on both sides of each slice of bread. As you butter the slices, fit each one into a cup of a muffin tin. Press the bread gently but firmly against the bottom and sides of the cup, and let the corners of each slice extend like points above the surface of the tin. Toast the bread in the middle of the oven for 8 to 10 minutes, or until it is crisp and lightly browned. Then turn the toast cups out on wire racks to cool while you prepare the creamed chipped beef.

CREAMED CHIPPED BEEF
4 tablespoons butter
¼ cup finely chopped onions
¼ cup flour
1 cup light cream
1 cup milk
4 to 5 ounces dried beef, sliced
   paper-thin, then torn into 1-inch
   pieces (about 2 cups)
2 tablespoons finely chopped fresh
   parsley
2 tablespoons dry sherry
1 tablespoon strained fresh lemon
   juice
⅛ teaspoon paprika

In a heavy 10- to 12-inch skillet, melt the 4 tablespoons of butter over moderate heat. Add the onions and cook for about 5 minutes, until they are soft and translucent but not brown. Add the flour and blend well. Stirring the mixture constantly with a wire whisk, pour in the cream and milk in a slow, thin stream and cook over high heat until the sauce comes to a boil, thickens lightly and is smooth.

Reduce the heat to low and simmer the sauce for 2 or 3 minutes to remove any taste of raw flour. Stir in the dried beef, parsley, sherry, lemon juice and paprika, and simmer for a minute or so longer to heat the beef through. Taste for seasoning.

Arrange pairs of toast cups on 4 individual heated serving plates and spoon the creamed chipped beef into the cups. Serve at once.

Stuffed Fresh Ham

To serve 8 to 10

1 cup soft fresh crumbs made from homemade-type white bread, pulverized in a blender or finely shredded with a fork
½ pound lean pork, finely ground
1 egg
½ cup finely chopped onions
¼ cup finely chopped fresh parsley

½ teaspoon finely chopped garlic
¼ teaspoon ground sage
½ teaspoon salt
Freshly ground black pepper
A 7- to 8-pound shank half of fresh ham, boned and trimmed of excess fat
1 cup apple butter *(page 107)*

Preheat the oven to 300°. First prepare the stuffing in the following fashion: Place the bread crumbs, ground pork, egg, onions, parsley, garlic, sage, salt and a few grindings of pepper in a deep bowl. Knead vigorously with both hands to combine the ingredients, then beat with a wooden spoon until the mixture is smooth and fluffy.

Spoon the stuffing into the cavity of the ham, packing it in as tightly as you can. To keep the stuffing in place, close the openings at both ends of the ham with small skewers and cord as if you were lacing a turkey or sew them tightly shut with heavy white thread. For the most predictable results, insert a meat thermometer at least 2 inches into the fleshiest part of the ham.

Place the ham, fat side up, on a rack in a shallow roasting pan and roast it uncovered in the middle of the oven for 4 hours, or until the juices run clear when the ham is pierced deeply with the point of a small skewer or sharp knife. A meat thermometer will register 165° to 170° when the ham is done.

Remove the thermometer if you have used one and, with a pastry brush, spread the apple butter evenly over the surface of the ham. Roast the ham for 30 minutes longer, or until the apple butter has formed a glaze. Then transfer the ham to a heated platter, remove the skewers or thread, and let the ham rest for 15 minutes for easier carving.

Meanwhile, skim as much fat as possible from the surface of the juices remaining in the pan. Taste for seasoning and pour the juices into a small bowl or sauceboat.

To serve, carve the ham vertically into ⅛-inch-thick slices and arrange the slices attractively on another heated platter. Present the gravy separately with the ham.

POULTRY & GAME BIRDS

Chicken-stuffed Onions, Shaker Style

To serve 4

1 tablespoon butter, softened,
plus 4 teaspoons butter, cut into
¼-inch bits
4 large onions, each about
3½ inches in diameter
1½ cups finely chopped cooked
chicken *(see chicken mousse,
page 48)*
½ cup finely chopped celery

2 tablespoons finely chopped fresh
parsley
½ teaspoon crumbled dried savory
½ teaspoon crumbled dried basil
¼ teaspoon crumbled dried thyme
⅛ teaspoon crumbled dried sage
leaves
1 teaspoon salt
Freshly ground black pepper
¼ cup heavy cream

Preheat the oven to 350°. With a pastry brush, spread the tablespoon of softened butter evenly over the bottom and sides of a shallow baking dish large enough to hold the onions in one layer. Set the dish aside.

Drop the onions into enough boiling water to cover them completely and cook briskly, uncovered, for about 10 minutes. Drain the onions in a sieve or colander and cut off the root ends with a small sharp knife. Slip off the papery outer skins. Cut a ¼-inch-thick slice off the top of each onion and, with a spoon, scoop out the center to leave a shell about ¼ inch thick. Discard the centers. Then invert the onion shells on paper towels to drain.

To make the stuffing, combine the chicken, celery, parsley, savory, basil, thyme, sage, salt and a few grindings of pepper in a bowl and toss them together gently but thoroughly with a spoon. Pour in the cream and stir until the stuffing is evenly moistened. Taste for seasoning.

Spoon the stuffing into the onion shells, dividing it evenly among them. Arrange the onions side by side in the buttered dish and dot the tops with the 4 teaspoons of butter bits. Bake in the middle of the oven for about 20 minutes, or until the onions are golden brown and tender. Serve at once from a heated platter.

Chicken Breasts and Ham with Sherried Cream Sauce

To serve 6

9 tablespoons butter
2 tablespoons finely chopped
    shallots
3 one-pound chicken breasts,
    halved, skinned and boned
1½ cups chicken stock, fresh or
    canned
¼ cup flour

½ cup heavy cream
2 tablespoons dry sherry
1 tablespoon finely chopped parsley
½ teaspoon salt
A pinch of ground white pepper
6 thin slices cooked country ham,
    plus 1 thin slice country ham cut
    in matchlike strips

In a heavy 10- to 12-inch skillet, melt 2 tablespoons of the butter over moderate heat. When the foam begins to subside, add the shallots and, stirring frequently, cook for 2 or 3 minutes, until they are soft and translucent but not brown. Add the chicken breasts and stock, and bring to a boil over high heat, meanwhile skimming off the foam and scum as they rise to the surface. Reduce the heat to low and simmer partially covered for about 10 minutes, or until the chicken feels firm to the touch. With a slotted spoon, transfer the chicken to a plate and drape it with foil to keep it warm. Set the stock aside.

Melt 3 tablespoons of the remaining butter in a 1- to 2-quart saucepan over moderate heat. Add the flour and mix to a paste. Then, stirring the mixture constantly with a wire whisk, pour in the reserved chicken stock and shallots, and cook over high heat until the sauce comes to a boil, thickens heavily and is smooth.

Whisking constantly, add the cream, sherry, parsley, salt and white pepper. Reduce the heat to low and simmer uncovered for 3 minutes to remove any taste of raw flour. Taste for seasoning.

While the sauce is simmering, melt the remaining 4 tablespoons of butter in a heavy 12-inch skillet over high heat. Add the ham slices and, turning them over frequently with kitchen tongs, cook for a few minutes to heat the ham through.

To serve, place the ham slices on six heated individual serving plates and set a chicken breast half on each slice. Pour the sauce over the chicken and ham, dividing it evenly among the portions. Garnish the top with the strips of ham and serve at once.

Chicken Potpie

To serve 6 to 8

A 5- to 6-pound roasting chicken,
    cut into 6 or 8 pieces
4 quarts water
2 medium-sized celery stalks,
    including the green leaves, cut
    into 3-inch pieces
¼ teaspoon crumbled dried saffron
    threads or ¼ teaspoon ground
    saffron
1 tablespoon plus 2 teaspoons salt

6 whole black peppercorns
½ cup coarsely chopped celery
2 medium-sized boiling potatoes,
    peeled and coarsely chopped
½ pound potpie squares (see
    homemade egg noodles, page 4)
2 tablespoons finely chopped fresh
    parsley
Freshly ground black pepper

In Pennsylvania Dutch cooking, potpies are pieces of noodle or baking-powder dough. They are boiled with meat and often potatoes to make rib-sticking potpie stews that are named for the kind of meat used. Thus, the following recipe made with chicken is called "chicken potpie" though it bears no resemblance to the pastry-encased potpies typical of other parts of the United States.

Combine the chicken and water in a heavy 6- to 8-quart casserole and bring to a boil over high heat, meanwhile skimming off the foam and scum as they rise to the surface. Add the pieces of celery, saffron, 1 tablespoon of salt and the peppercorns, and reduce the heat to low. Simmer partially covered for about 1 hour, or until the chicken shows no resistance when a thigh is pierced deeply with a small sharp knife.

With a slotted spoon, transfer the chicken to a plate. Strain the stock through a fine sieve and return 2 quarts to the casserole. (Reserve the remaining stock for another use.) With a small sharp knife, remove the skin from the chicken and cut the meat from the bones. Discard the skin and bones; slice the meat into 1-inch pieces and set aside.

Add the chopped celery, potatoes and the remaining 2 teaspoons of salt to the casserole and bring to a boil over high heat. Drop in the potpie squares and stir briefly, then cook briskly, uncovered, for about 15 minutes, until the noodles are tender. Stir in the reserved chicken and parsley and cook for a minute or so to heat them through. Taste and season with more salt if desired and a few grindings of pepper.

To serve, ladle the chicken potpie into heated individual bowls.

Chicken Mousse

To serve 4 to 6

1 tablespoon vegetable oil
¼ cup cold water
1 envelope unflavored gelatin
2 cups finely chopped cooked
  chicken *(see note below)*
½ cup finely chopped celery
¼ cup finely chopped onions

⅓ cup heavy cream, chilled
1½ cups freshly made mayonnaise
  (page 7), or substitute
  unsweetened bottled mayonnaise
¼ cup tarragon vinegar
2 teaspoons salt
⅛ teaspoon ground hot red pepper
  (cayenne)

Brush the inside of a 1-quart soufflé dish or ring mold with vegetable oil, and invert the mold on paper towels to drain.

Pour the water into a heatproof measuring cup and sprinkle the gelatin over it. Let the gelatin soften for 2 or 3 minutes, then set the cup in a small skillet of simmering water and, stirring constantly, cook over low heat until the gelatin dissolves. Remove the cup of gelatin from the skillet and set aside.

Meanwhile, put the chicken, celery and onions through the finest blade of a food grinder. In a chilled bowl, whip the cream with a wire whisk or a rotary or electric beater until it is stiff enough to stand in unwavering peaks on the beater when it is lifted from the bowl.

Combine the mayonnaise, vinegar and the reserved gelatin in a deep bowl and mix well. Stir in the ground chicken and vegetables, the salt and cayenne, then fold the whipped cream into the mixture with a rubber spatula. Taste for seasoning.

Spoon the mixture into the oiled mold, spreading it evenly and smoothing the top with the spatula. Cover tightly with foil or plastic wrap and refrigerate for at least 3 hours, or until the mousse is firm.

To unmold and serve the mousse, run a sharp knife around the sides of the mold and dip the bottom in hot water for a few seconds. Place a chilled serving plate upside down over the mold and, grasping plate and mold together firmly, quickly invert them. Rap the plate on a table and the mousse should slide out easily.

NOTE: If you do not have cooked chicken meat on hand, prepare it by poaching a whole 1-pound chicken breast, a small sliced onion, 2 celery tops, a small bay leaf and a teaspoon of salt in 2 cups of water. Bring to a boil, cover and simmer over low heat for about 20 minutes. Remove the chicken and when cool, bone, skin and chop it. You should have about 2 cups of chopped chicken.

Batter-fried Chicken

To serve 4

1 egg	1½ teaspoons salt
½ cup milk	Vegetable oil for deep frying
1 cup unsifted flour	A 3- to 3½-pound chicken, cut
1 teaspoon double-acting baking	into 8 serving pieces
powder	2 teaspoons paprika

In a deep bowl, beat the egg and milk lightly together with a wire whisk. Combine the flour, baking powder and ½ teaspoon of the salt, and add them to the egg mixture a few tablespoonfuls at a time, stirring gently after each addition. Stir until the batter is smooth, but do not beat or over-mix. Set the batter aside at room temperature for about 30 minutes.

Preheat the oven to its lowest setting. Then line a large shallow baking dish with a double thickness of paper towels and place it in the middle of the oven.

Pour vegetable oil into a deep fryer or large heavy saucepan to a depth of 2 to 3 inches and heat the oil until it reaches a temperature of 360° on a deep-frying thermometer.

Meanwhile, pat the pieces of chicken completely dry with paper towels and season them evenly on both sides with the paprika and the remaining teaspoon of salt.

Dip the chicken drumsticks and thighs into the batter, one at a time, and when they are thoroughly coated place them in a deep-frying basket. Lower the basket into the hot oil and deep-fry the chicken for 12 to 15 minutes, turning the drumsticks and thighs frequently with kitchen tongs so that they color richly and evenly.

To test for doneness, after 12 minutes lift a thigh out of the oil and pierce it deeply with the point of a small skewer or sharp knife. The juice that trickles out should be pale yellow; if it is still tinged with pink, deep-fry the chicken for 1 or 2 minutes longer. Transfer the drumsticks and thighs to the paper-lined dish to drain, and keep them warm in the oven.

Then dip the wings and breasts into the batter, place them in the deep-frying basket, and lower it into the oil. Fry the white-meat pieces for about 7 or 8 minutes, then drain them on the paper-lined dish.

Arrange the chicken attractively on a heated platter and serve at once.

Chicken Croquettes

To serve 6

1½ pounds chicken breasts
2½ teaspoons salt
1 quart water
1 medium-sized onion, peeled and
  coarsely chopped
1 medium-sized bay leaf, crumbled
4 whole black peppercorns
10 tablespoons butter
¼ cup finely chopped onions
¼ cup finely chopped celery
¼ cup finely chopped fresh parsley
1 tablespoon strained fresh lemon
  juice

A pinch of ground hot red pepper
  (cayenne)
½ cup flour
2 cups fresh soft crumbs made from
  homemade-type white bread,
  pulverized in a blender or finely
  shredded with a fork
2 eggs lightly beaten with ¼ cup
  milk
Vegetable oil for deep frying
¾ cup light cream
¼ teaspoon ground nutmeg,
  preferably freshly grated

Combine the chicken breasts, 1 teaspoon of the salt and the water in a heavy 3- to 4-quart saucepan. The water should cover the chicken by at least 1 inch; add more if necessary. Bring to a boil over high heat, meanwhile skimming off the foam and scum that rise to the surface. Add the coarsely chopped onion, bay leaf and peppercorns, reduce the heat to low, and partially cover the pan. Simmer for about 20 minutes, or until the chicken is firm to the touch.

Transfer the chicken to a plate. Strain the cooking liquid through a fine sieve into a bowl; measure and reserve 2 cups. With a small sharp knife, remove the skin from the breasts and cut the meat away from the bones. Discard the skin and bones. Then put the chicken through the finest blade of a meat grinder or chop it as fine as possible. Set aside.

In a heavy 8- to 10-inch skillet, melt 2 tablespoons of the butter over moderate heat. When the foam begins to subside, add the finely chopped onions and celery and, stirring frequently, cook for about 5 minutes, or until the vegetables are soft but not brown. With a rubber spatula, scrape the contents of the skillet into a deep bowl. Add the chicken, parsley, lemon juice and red pepper, and stir vigorously with a wooden spoon until all the ingredients are thoroughly blended.

In the same skillet, melt the remaining 8 tablespoons of butter over moderate heat. When the foam subsides, add the flour and mix well. Stirring the mixture constantly with a wire whisk, pour in the reserved 2 cups of chicken stock in a slow, thin stream and cook over high heat until the sauce comes to a boil, thickens heavily and is smooth. Reduce the heat to low and simmer for 2 or 3 minutes.

Add 1 cup of the sauce to the chicken mixture, stir together thoroughly, and taste for seasoning. Cover the bowl with foil or plastic wrap and refrigerate the chicken for at least 1 hour. Let the remaining sauce cool to room temperature, cover the skillet tightly and refrigerate until ready to serve.

To shape the croquettes, divide the chilled chicken mixture into 12 equal portions. Pat and roll each portion into a conical croquette about 2 inches high and 2½ inches in diameter across the bottom. One at a time, roll the croquettes in the bread crumbs, immerse them in the beaten egg-and-milk mixture, then roll them again in crumbs to coat all sides evenly. Stand the croquettes on wax paper and refrigerate them for at least 30 minutes to firm the coating.

Preheat the oven to its lowest setting. At the same time, line a large shallow baking pan with a double thickness of paper towels and place it in the center of the oven.

Pour vegetable oil into a deep fryer or large heavy saucepan to a depth of about 3 inches and heat the oil until it reaches a temperature of 375° on a deep-frying thermometer.

Deep-fry the croquettes 3 or 4 at a time, turning them with a slotted spoon, for about 5 minutes, or until they are golden brown. When they are done, transfer the croquettes to the paper-lined pan and keep them warm in the oven while you deep-fry the rest.

Return the skillet of sauce to low heat and stir with a wire whisk until it is heated through. Whisking constantly, gradually pour in the cream in a thin stream and simmer until the sauce is smooth. Stir in the nutmeg and taste for seasoning.

To serve, arrange the croquettes attractively on a heated platter. Present the sauce separately in a bowl or sauceboat.

Chicken Stoltzfus

To serve 6 to 8

A 5- to 6-pound roasting chicken,
cut into 6 or 8 pieces
4 quarts water
2 medium-sized celery stalks,
including the green leaves, cut
into 3-inch pieces
¼ teaspoon crumbled dried saffron
threads or ¼ teaspoon ground
saffron
1 tablespoon plus ½ teaspoon salt

6 whole black peppercorns
1½ cups plus ¾ cup unsifted
flour
6 tablespoons vegetable shortening,
cut into ¼-inch bits
3 tablespoons butter, chilled and
cut into ¼-inch bits, plus
12 tablespoons butter
2 cups light cream
¼ cup finely chopped fresh parsley

Combine the chicken and water in a heavy 6- to 8-quart casserole and
bring to a boil over high heat, skimming off the foam and scum as they
rise to the surface. Add the celery, saffron, 1 tablespoon of the salt and
the peppercorns, and reduce the heat to low. Cover the casserole partially
and simmer for about 1 hour, or until the chicken shows no resistance
when a thigh is pierced deeply with the point of a small sharp knife.

Meanwhile, place 1½ cups of flour and the remaining ½ teaspoon
of salt in a deep bowl. Add the vegetable shortening and 3 tablespoons
of butter bits and, with your fingers, rub the flour and fat together until
they form a smooth dough that can be gathered into a compact ball.
Wrap the ball in wax paper and refrigerate for about 1 hour.

When the chicken has cooked its allotted time, transfer the pieces to a
plate with a slotted spoon. Strain the stock through a fine sieve, measure
it and set aside 6 cups. (Reserve the remaining stock for another use.)
With a small sharp knife, remove the skin from the chicken and cut the
meat from the bones. Discard the skin and bones; slice the meat into 2-
or 3-inch pieces and set aside.

About half an hour before serving, preheat the oven to 350°. Place the
ball of dough on a lightly floured surface and roll it out into a rectangle
about ⅛ inch thick.

With a pastry wheel or small sharp knife, cut the dough into 1-inch
squares. Gather the scraps into a ball, roll out as before, and cut as many
more squares as you can. Arrange the squares about ½ inch apart on ungreased baking sheets and bake in the middle of the oven for 12 to 15 minutes, or until they are golden brown.

While the pastry bakes, melt the remaining 12 tablespoons of butter
over moderate heat in a heavy 5- to 6-quart casserole. When the foam begins to subside, add the remaining ¾ cup of flour and mix the flour and
butter together thoroughly. Stirring the mixture constantly with a wire

whisk, pour in the reserved 6 cups of chicken stock and the cream in a slow thin stream and cook over high heat until the sauce comes to a boil, thickens lightly and is smooth.

Reduce the heat to low and simmer for 2 or 3 minutes to remove any taste of raw flour. Then stir in the reserved chicken pieces and the chopped parsley and simmer for a few minutes longer to heat the chicken through. Taste for seasoning.

To serve, ladle the chicken mixture onto a heated platter and arrange the pastries attractively around it or on top.

Stewed Chicken with Parsley Dumplings

To serve 4

CHICKEN

A 3½- to 4-pound chicken, cut
    into 8 serving pieces
¼ cup flour
⅓ cup vegetable oil
1 large onion, peeled and sliced
    crosswise into ¼-inch-thick
    rounds
6 cups chicken stock, fresh or
canned
¼ cup cider vinegar
1 celery stalk, including the green
    leaves, cut crosswise into 4 pieces
1 medium-sized bay leaf
¼ teaspoon crumbled dried sage
    leaves
2 teaspoons salt
Freshly ground black pepper

Pat the chicken dry with paper towels. Place the flour in a paper bag, add the chicken, and shake vigorously to coat the pieces evenly.

In a heavy 4- to 5-quart casserole or Dutch oven at least 10 inches in diameter, heat the oil over moderate heat until a light haze forms above it. Brown 3 or 4 pieces of chicken at a time, starting them skin side down, and turning them frequently with tongs. Regulate the heat so that the pieces color richly and evenly without burning. As they brown, transfer the pieces to a plate.

Drop the onion slices into the fat remaining in the casserole and, stirring frequently, cook for about 5 minutes. When the onions are soft and translucent but not brown, return the chicken and the liquid that has accumulated around it to the casserole. Add the chicken stock, vinegar, celery, bay leaf, sage, 2 teaspoons of salt and a few grindings of pepper,

Continued on next page

and bring to a boil over high heat. Reduce the heat to low, cover partially and simmer for 45 minutes, or until the bird is almost tender and its thigh shows only the slightest resistance when pierced deeply with the point of a small sharp knife. Pick out and discard the celery and bay leaf.

DUMPLINGS

2 cups unsifted flour

4 teaspoons double-acting baking powder

1 teaspoon salt

¼ cup finely chopped fresh parsley

2 tablespoons vegetable shortening, cut into ½-inch bits

1 cup milk

Meanwhile, prepare the dumpling batter in the following fashion: Combine the flour, baking powder, 1 teaspoon of salt and the parsley in a deep bowl. Add the vegetable shortening and, with your fingertips, rub the flour and fat together until they look like flakes of coarse meal. Add the milk and beat vigorously with a spoon until the batter is smooth.

When the chicken has cooked its allotted time, drop the dumpling mixture on top by the tablespoonful. Cover the casserole tightly and simmer undisturbed for about 10 minutes longer. The dumplings are done when they are puffed and fluffy and a cake tester inserted in the center of a dumpling comes out clean.

With a slotted spoon remove the dumplings and place them on a plate. Transfer the stewed chicken to a heated bowl or a deep platter, then arrange the dumplings on top. Serve at once.

Braised Pheasant with Sauerkraut

To serve 4

2 pounds fresh sauerkraut
4 slices lean bacon
1 cup finely chopped onions
1 tablespoon finely chopped garlic
1 cup dry white wine
1 cup water
1 medium-sized carrot, scraped and
    coarsely grated

1 teaspoon freshly ground black
    pepper
4 whole juniper berries and 1
    medium-sized bay leaf, wrapped
    together in cheesecloth
A 3- to 3½-pound oven-ready
    pheasant
2 tablespoons butter
1 tablespoon vegetable oil

Drain the sauerkraut, wash it thoroughly under cold running water and let it soak in a pot of water for about 15 minutes. Then, a handful at a time, squeeze the sauerkraut completely dry. Set aside.

Preheat the oven to 350°. In a heavy 6- to 8-quart casserole, fry the bacon over moderate heat, turning the slices frequently with tongs until they are crisp and brown and have rendered all their fat. As soon as each slice is brown, transfer it to a paper towel to drain.

Pour off all but about 3 tablespoons of the fat remaining in the casserole and add the onions and garlic. Stirring frequently, cook over moderate heat for about 5 minutes, or until they are soft and translucent but not brown. Stir in the wine, water, carrot and black pepper. Add the sauerkraut and toss the mixture about with a fork until all the ingredients are well combined. Tuck the cheesecloth-wrapped juniper berries and bay leaf down into the sauerkraut mixture.

Lay the reserved bacon slices on top of the sauerkraut and cover the casserole lightly with both a sheet of foil and the lid. Bring to a boil over high heat, then braise in the lower third of the oven for 1½ hours.

Wash the pheasant briefly under cold running water and pat it dry inside and out with paper towels. Truss the bird securely.

In a heavy 10- to 12-inch skillet, melt the butter with the oil over moderate heat. Add the pheasant and, turning it about with tongs, brown it as evenly as possible on all sides. Regulate the heat so that the pheasant colors richly without burning.

When the sauerkraut mixture has cooked its allotted time, transfer about half of it to a bowl, leaving a 1-inch layer or so in the bottom of the casserole. Set the pheasant in the middle of the pot and spread the sauerkraut from the bowl over and around it. Cover the casserole again with foil as well as the lid and braise for 2 hours longer, or until the bird is tender but not falling apart.

Serve at once directly from the casserole. Or place the pheasant in the center of a large heated platter, pick out and discard the cheesecloth bag, and mound the sauerkraut around the bird.

Roast Pheasant with Filbert Stuffing and Currant Sauce

To serve 4

9 tablespoons butter, plus
  6 tablespoons butter, softened
4 to 5 slices homemade-type white
  bread, trimmed of all crusts and
  cut into ¼-inch cubes (about
  2 cups)
½ cup finely chopped celery
1 cup finely chopped onions
½ cup filberts, pulverized in a
  blender or with a nut grinder
¼ teaspoon ground sage
1 teaspoon salt
Freshly ground black pepper

A 3- to 3½-pound oven-ready
  pheasant
2 tablespoons thin strips orange
  peel, each cut about ⅛ inch wide and
  1 inch long
1 tablespoon thin strips lemon peel,
  each cut about ⅛ inch wide and
  1 inch long
1¼ cups chicken stock, fresh or
  canned
2 tablespoons currant jelly
2 tablespoons port
1 tablespoon cornstarch

Preheat the oven to 400°. To make the stuffing, melt 8 tablespoons of the butter over moderate heat in a heavy 8- to 10-inch skillet. When the foam begins to subside, add the bread cubes and stir until they are crisp and brown. With a slotted spoon, transfer the cubes to a deep bowl.

Add 1 tablespoon of butter to that remaining in the skillet and drop in the celery and ½ cup of the onions. Stirring frequently, cook over moderate heat for about 5 minutes, or until the vegetables are soft but not brown. With a rubber spatula, scrape the entire contents of the skillet over the bread cubes. Add the filberts, sage, salt and a few grindings of pepper, and toss together gently but thoroughly.

Wash the pheasant quickly under cold running water and pat it dry inside and out with paper towels. Fill the cavity loosely with the stuffing and close the opening by lacing it with small skewers and cord or sewing it with heavy white thread. Fasten the neck skin to the back of the pheasant with a skewer and truss the bird neatly. With a pastry brush, spread 4 tablespoons of the softened butter evenly over the surface of the bird.

Lay the bird on its side on a rack set in a shallow roasting pan. Roast the pheasant in the middle of the oven for 10 minutes. Turn it over, brush it with the remaining 2 tablespoons of softened butter, and roast it for 10 minutes longer. Then turn the bird breast side up and baste it with the fat that has accumulated in the pan. Continue roasting for 20 to 30 minutes, or until it is golden brown, basting the bird with its pan juices every 10 minutes. To test for doneness, pierce a thigh with the point of a small skewer or with a sharp knife; the juices that trickle out should be clear yellow. If they are still tinged with pink, roast the pheasant for about 5 minutes longer.

Meanwhile drop the strips of the orange and lemon peel into enough boiling water to immerse them completely and cook briskly, uncovered, for 5 minutes. Drain in a sieve and run cold water over the peel to set the color. Reserve the peel.

When the pheasant has roasted for its allotted time, transfer it to a heated platter. Remove the trussing string and drape the platter loosely with foil to keep the bird warm while you prepare the sauce.

With a large spoon, skim as much fat as possible from the surface of the liquid remaining in the roasting pan. Add 1 cup of the chicken stock, the remaining ½ cup of onions, the currant jelly and port. Bring to a boil over high heat, stirring constantly and scraping in the brown particles that cling to the bottom and sides of the pan. Reduce the heat to low and simmer uncovered for about 5 minutes.

Dissolve the cornstarch in the remaining ¼ cup of chicken stock and stir it into the simmering sauce. Cook, still stirring, until the sauce comes to a boil, thickens and clears. Strain the sauce through a fine sieve into a sauceboat or gravy bowl and stir in the reserved orange and lemon peel. Taste for seasoning.

Serve the pheasant at once, garnished, if you like, with additional slices of orange peel and accompanied by the sauce.

Braised Wild Duck

To serve 4

4 one-pound oven-ready wild ducks	1 cup water
2 teaspoons salt	2 small bay leaves
1 teaspoon freshly ground black pepper	4 whole cloves
¼ pound lean salt pork, diced	4 tablespoons butter
1 cup finely chopped onions	¼ cup finely chopped shallots
½ cup finely chopped celery	⅓ cup flour
1½ cups dry red wine	2 tablespoons finely grated fresh orange peel
1½ cups chicken stock, fresh or canned	¼ cup brandy

Preheat the oven to 325°. Wash the ducks briefly under cold running water and pat them completely dry inside and out with paper towels. With a sharp heavy knife cut off the wing tips and discard them. Sprinkle the cavities of the ducks with 1 teaspoon of the salt and ½ teaspoon of the pepper, dividing the seasoning evenly among them.

In a heavy 10- to 12-inch skillet, fry the salt pork over moderate heat until it is crisp and brown and has rendered all its fat. Remove the dice from the pan and discard them.

Brown the ducks, two at a time, in the fat remaining in the skillet. Turn the birds frequently with tongs and regulate the heat so that they color richly and as evenly as possible without burning. As they brown, arrange the ducks side by side in a heavy casserole large enough to hold them comfortably and equipped with a tight-fitting lid.

Add the onions and celery to the skillet and, stirring frequently, cook over moderate heat for about 5 minutes, or until they are soft but not brown. Add the wine, chicken stock, water, bay leaves and cloves, and bring to a boil over high heat, meanwhile scraping in any browned particles clinging to the bottom and sides of the pan. With a rubber spatula, scrape the entire contents of the skillet over the ducks. Cover the casserole tightly and braise the ducks in the middle of the oven for about 1 hour, or until their drumsticks feel soft when prodded with a finger.

Transfer the ducks to a platter while you prepare the sauce. Strain the cooking liquid through a fine sieve set over a bowl, pressing down hard on the onions and celery to extract all their juices before discarding the pulp, the bay leaves and the cloves. Let the liquid rest for a few minutes, then skim off and discard the surface fat.

In a heavy 3- to 4-quart saucepan, melt the butter over moderate heat. When the foam begins to subside, add the shallots and stir for 2 or 3 minutes, until they are soft but not brown. Add the flour and mix well. Stirring the mixture constantly with a wire whisk, pour in the strained cooking liquid and cook over high heat, still stirring, until the sauce comes to a boil, thickens lightly and is smooth. Reduce the heat to low and simmer for about 5 minutes to remove any taste of raw flour. Stir in the grated orange peel, the remaining teaspoon of salt and ½ teaspoon of black pepper.

Warm the brandy in a small saucepan over low heat, ignite it with a match and pour it flaming into the sauce. Slide the pan back and forth until the flames die, then taste the sauce for seasoning.

With a small sharp knife, remove the skin from the ducks and cut the meat off the bones into large pieces. Discard the skin and bones. Add the meat to the sauce and simmer over low heat for a few minutes, or until the pieces of duck are heated through. Serve the braised wild ducks at once from a deep, heated platter.

Roast Duck with Apricot-Rice Stuffing

To serve 4

2 cups water
2 teaspoons salt
1 cup long-grain white rice, not the
   converted variety
24 dried apricots (about 1½ cups),
   quartered
Freshly ground black pepper
A 5- to 6-pound duck

2 cups chicken stock, fresh or
   canned
½ cup finely chopped onions
½ teaspoon finely chopped garlic
⅛ teaspoon crumbled dried thyme
2 tablespoons apricot preserves
2 tablespoons cornstarch combined
   with 2 tablespoons cold water

Preheat the oven to 425°. To prepare the stuffing, bring the 2 cups of water and 1 teaspoon of the salt to a boil over high heat in a small saucepan. Pour in the rice, stir once or twice, and reduce the heat to low. Cover the pan tightly and simmer for 10 minutes. Drain the rice in a sieve and transfer it to a bowl. Add the apricots and a liberal grinding of black pepper and mix well.

Wash the duck quickly under cold running water and pat it dry inside and out with paper towels. Rub the inside of the duck with the remaining teaspoon of salt and a few grindings of black pepper. For a crisper skin, prick the surface around the thighs, the back and the lower part of the breast with the tip of a sharp knife.

Fill the cavity of the duck loosely with the stuffing and close the opening by lacing it with small skewers and cord or sewing it with heavy white thread. Fasten the neck skin to the back of the duck with a skewer and truss the bird neatly.

Place the duck breast side up on a rack set in a large shallow pan and roast it in the middle of the oven for 20 minutes. Pour off the fat from the roasting pan or draw it off with a bulb baster. Then reduce the heat to 350° and roast for about 1 hour longer.

To test for doneness pierce the thigh of the bird deeply with the point of a small skewer or a sharp knife. The juice that trickles out should be a clear yellow; if it is still slightly tinged with pink, roast the duck for another 5 to 10 minutes. Transfer the bird to a heated serving platter and discard the string and skewers. Let the roast duck rest for about 10 minutes for easier carving.

Meanwhile, prepare the sauce in the following way: Pour off all but about 3 tablespoons of the fat remaining in the roasting pan and add the chicken stock, onions, garlic and thyme. Bring to a boil over high heat, stirring constantly and scraping in the brown particles that cling to the bottom and sides of the pan. Reduce the heat to low and simmer uncovered for about 5 minutes.

Add the apricot preserve and the cornstarch-water mixture and, still stirring, cook over low heat until the sauce comes to a boil and thickens lightly. Strain the sauce through a fine sieve into a sauceboat or gravy bowl, pressing down hard on the onions with the back of a spoon to extract all their juices before discarding the pulp. Taste for seasoning.

Serve the duck at once, accompanied by the sauce. If you like, you may garnish the duck with dried apricots that have been simmered in water to cover for 30 minutes, or until tender, and thoroughly drained.

Broiled Quail with Mustard Butter

To serve 4

Eight 4- to 5-ounce oven-ready quail
½ pound butter, melted
2 tablespoons prepared mustard
2 teaspoons strained fresh lemon
   juice

Salt
Freshly ground black pepper
8 thin slices homemade-type white
   bread, cut into 4-inch rounds and
   fried in 8 tablespoons butter
Watercress

Cut each quail down the back from neck to tail with a large knife or poultry shears. Spread the birds out skin side up and, with the flat of a cleaver or wooden mallet, break the curved rib bones so that the birds lie flat. Twist the wing tips under the shoulders.

Preheat the broiler to its highest setting. Combine the melted butter, mustard and lemon juice in a shallow baking dish. Dip the quail, one at a time, into the butter mixture and, when they are thoroughly saturated, arrange them skin side down on the broiler rack. Sprinkle with salt and a few grindings of pepper.

Broil the birds about 4 inches from the heat for about 5 minutes. Then brush them again with the butter mixture and turn them over with tongs. Brush the quail with the remaining butter, sprinkle generously with salt and pepper, and broil about 5 minutes longer. Watch the birds carefully for any sign of burning and regulate the broiler heat accordingly. The quail should be crisp and golden brown when they are done.

To serve, arrange the fried bread rounds on a heated platter and place a quail on top of each one. Pour the broiler pan juices over the birds, garnish the platter with crisp watercress, and serve at once.

FISH & SHELLFISH

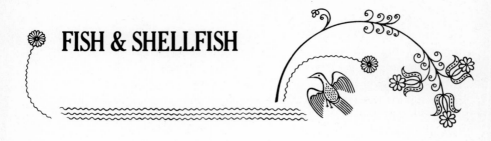

Batter-fried Bluegills

To serve 4

Vegetable oil for deep frying
½ cup cake flour, not the self-
   rising variety
2 tablespoons cornstarch
½ teaspoon salt
½ teaspoon freshly ground black

pepper
1 egg yolk
½ cup water
1 egg white
1 pound bluegill or other sunfish
   fillets, skinned
1 lemon, quartered

Bluegills are a kind of sunfish, native to the Eastern Heartland, but now used for stocking lakes and ponds nationwide. A sought-after sport and food fish, sunfish are known as bream in the South.

Pour the vegetable oil into a deep fryer or large heavy saucepan to a depth of about 3 inches and heat the oil until it reaches a temperature of 375° on a deep-frying thermometer.

Meanwhile, prepare the batter in the following fashion: Combine the flour, cornstarch, salt and pepper, and sift them together onto a plate or a sheet of wax paper. With a wire whisk, beat the egg yolk and water to a smooth cream and then incorporate the flour mixture, a few tablespoons at a time. Just before using the batter, beat the egg white with a wire whisk or a rotary or electric beater until it is stiff enough to stand in un-wavering peaks on the beater when it is lifted from the bowl. Scoop the egg white over the batter and fold it in gently with a rubber spatula.

Pat the fish fillets dry with paper towels. Pick up one fillet with tongs, immerse it in the batter, and drop it into the oil. Deep-fry 4 or 5 fillets at a time, turning them with a slotted spoon for 3 minutes, or until golden brown. As they brown, transfer the fillets to paper towels to drain.

Arrange the fillets attractively on a heated platter and serve them at once, accompanied by the lemon quarters.

Fried Lake Perch Fillets with Tartar Sauce

To serve 4

TARTAR SAUCE

1½ cups freshly made mayonnaise
  (page 7), or substitute 1½
  cups unsweetened bottled
  mayonnaise
¼ cup finely grated onion
¼ cup finely cut fresh dill

3 tablespoons strained fresh lemon
  juice
1 tablespoon finely chopped fresh
  parsley
2 teaspoons prepared mustard
½ teaspoon salt

To prepare the tartar sauce, combine the mayonnaise, onion, dill, lemon juice, parsley, mustard and ½ teaspoon of salt in a deep bowl and stir until all the ingredients are well blended. Cover the bowl tightly with foil or plastic wrap and refrigerate the tartar sauce for at least 1 hour before serving. (Tightly covered and refrigerated, it can safely be kept for 1 or 2 days.)

FISH

8 three-ounce lake perch fillets
½ teaspoon salt

½ cup flour
4 tablespoons butter
2 tablespoons vegetable oil

Just before serving, wash the lake perch fillets briefly under cold running water and pat them completely dry with paper towels. Sprinkle the fish on both sides with ½ teaspoon of salt, then roll the fillets in the flour to coat them evenly. Vigorously shake off the excess flour.

In a heavy 10- to 12-inch skillet (preferably one with a nonstick surface) melt the butter with the oil over moderate heat. When the foam begins to subside, add the fillets and fry them for 2 or 3 minutes on each side, or until they are golden brown and flake easily when prodded gently with a fork.

Arrange the fillets attractively on a heated platter and serve at once. Present the tartar sauce separately in a bowl.

Mushroom-stuffed Halibut Steak

To serve 4 to 6

1 tablespoon butter, softened, plus
    5 tablespoons butter, cut into
    ¼-inch bits, plus 2 tablespoons
    butter, melted
2 two-pound halibut steaks, cut
    about 1½ inches thick
½ teaspoon salt
½ cup finely chopped onions
½ cup finely chopped fresh
    mushrooms

½ cup soft fresh crumbs made
    from homemade-type white
    bread, pulverized in a blender or
    finely shredded with a fork
⅓ cup heavy cream
¼ cup finely chopped fresh parsley
⅛ teaspoon crumbled dried thyme
1 teaspoon strained fresh lemon
    juice
Freshly ground black pepper

Preheat the oven to 425°. With a pastry brush, spread the tablespoon of softened butter evenly over the bottom of a baking-serving dish at least 2 inches deep and wide enough to hold one of the halibut steaks comfortably. Pat the halibut steaks completely dry with paper towels and season them on both sides with the salt. Set the steaks aside while you prepare the mushroom stuffing.

In a heavy 8- to 10-inch skillet, melt 4 tablespoons of the butter bits over moderate heat. When the foam begins to subside, add the onions and, stirring frequently, cook for about 5 minutes, until they are soft and translucent but not brown.

Add the mushrooms and, still stirring from time to time, cook for 5 to 10 minutes but do not let them brown. When the moisture in the pan has evaporated, add the crumbs and stir until golden. Then stir in the cream, parsley, thyme, lemon juice and a few grindings of pepper, and remove the pan from the heat. Taste for seasoning.

Place one of the halibut steaks in the buttered baking dish and spread the mushroom mixture evenly over it. Set the second steak on top and dot it with the remaining tablespoon of butter bits.

Bake in the middle of the oven for about 30 minutes, basting the steaks every 10 minutes or so with the 2 tablespoons of melted butter and the liquids that accumulate in the dish. The halibut is done when it feels firm to the touch. Serve at once, directly from the baking dish.

Poached Salmon Steaks with Mousseline Sauce

To serve 6

POACHING LIQUID
2 quarts water
1 cup dry white wine
½ cup coarsely chopped onions
½ cup coarsely chopped leeks,
 including the green tops,
 thoroughly washed to remove any
 sand
¼ cup coarsely chopped celery,
including the leaves
1 medium-sized carrot, scraped and
 coarsely chopped
2 tablespoons finely chopped fresh
 parsley
1 small bay leaf, crumbled
¼ teaspoon crumbled dried thyme
1 tablespoon salt
1 teaspoon whole black peppercorns

First prepare the poaching liquid in the following fashion: Combine the water, wine, onions, leeks, celery, carrot, parsley, bay leaf, thyme, 1 tablespoon of salt and the peppercorns in a 4- to 5-quart enameled pot and bring to a boil over high heat. Reduce the heat to low, cover partially and simmer for 30 minutes. Strain the poaching liquid through a fine sieve into a heavy skillet at least 12 inches in diameter and 2½ inches deep.

SALMON
6 salmon steaks, cut 1 inch
thick and each weighing about
¾ pound

Arrange the salmon steaks side by side in the poaching liquid. Cover the skillet tightly and bring to a simmer over moderate heat. Immediately reduce the heat to low and simmer gently for about 10 minutes, or until the fish flakes easily when prodded gently with a fork. With a slotted spoon, transfer the salmon steaks to a heated platter.

MOUSSELINE SAUCE
½ pound unsalted butter, cut into
 ¼-inch bits
3 egg yolks
2 tablespoons cold water
3 tablespoons strained fresh lemon
juice
1 teaspoon salt
A pinch of ground hot red pepper
 (cayenne)
½ cup heavy cream, chilled

Meanwhile, make the hollandaise base for the mousseline sauce. In a small heavy saucepan, melt the butter over low heat, being careful not to let it brown.

In a heavy 2-quart enameled saucepan, beat the egg yolks and water vigorously together with a wire whisk until they are foamy. Place the egg mixture over the lowest possible heat and continue whisking until it

Continued on next page

thickens to the consistency of heavy cream. Do not let the eggs come anywhere near a boil or they will curdle.

Still whisking constantly, pour in the clear hot butter as slowly as possible, discarding the milky solids that will settle at the bottom of the pan. Continue to beat until the sauce thickens heavily, then add the lemon juice, the teaspoon of salt and the red pepper, and taste for seasoning. Set the hollandaise sauce aside to cool to lukewarm.

Just before serving, pour the cream into a chilled bowl. With a wire whisk or a rotary or electric beater, whip the cream until it is stiff enough to stand in unwavering peaks on the beater when it is lifted from the bowl. With a rubber spatula, scoop the whipped cream over the cooled hollandaise sauce and fold them toegther gently but thoroughly. Pour the mousseline sauce into a sauceboat or serving bowl and present it separately with the salmon.

Barbecued Stuffed Coho Salmon

To serve 6 to 8

1½ cups dry white wine
½ cup strained fresh lemon juice
½ cup plus 1 tablespoon vegetable oil
1 medium-sized onion, peeled and thinly sliced
3 medium-sized garlic cloves, crushed with the side of a cleaver or a large heavy knife
3 sprigs fresh parsley
1 teaspoon ground ginger
½ teaspoon crumbled dried thyme
¼ teaspoon Tabasco sauce
1 teaspoon salt
¼ teaspoon freshly ground black

pepper
A 5- to 5½-pound coho or other salmon, cleaned and with head and tail removed
1 cup freshly cooked rice, made from ½ cup long-grain white rice, not the converted variety
¼ cup finely chopped scallions, including 2 inches of the green tops
¼ cup finely chopped fresh parsley
The peel of ½ lemon, cut into matchlike strips
1 lemon, cut crosswise into ¼-inch-thick rounds

First prepare the marinade in the following manner: Combine the wine, lemon juice, ½ cup of the oil, the onion, garlic, parsley sprigs, ginger, thyme, Tabasco, salt and pepper in a small enameled saucepan and, stirring occasionally, bring to a boil over high heat. Pour the marinade into an enameled casserole or roasting pan large enough to hold the salmon comfortably, and set it aside to cool to room temperature.

Wash the salmon inside and out under cold running water and pat it dry with paper towels. With a sharp knife, score both sides of the fish by making four or five evenly spaced diagonal slits about 4 inches long and ¼ inch deep. Place the salmon in the cooled marinade and turn it over to moisten it evenly.

Cover the pan tightly with foil or plastic wrap and marinate at room temperature for about 3 hours, or in the refrigerator for about 6 hours, turning the fish occasionally.

Light a layer of briquettes in a charcoal broiler and let them burn until a white ash appears on the surface, or preheat the broiler of your stove to its highest setting.

Transfer the salmon to paper towels and pat it completely dry with more paper towels. Strain the marinade through a fine sieve set over a bowl. To prepare the stuffing, combine the rice, scallions, chopped parsley and lemon strips in a small bowl. Pour in ¼ cup of the strained marinade and mix well. Set the remaining marinade aside.

Loosely fill the salmon with the stuffing, then close the opening with small skewers and kitchen cord. With a pastry brush, spread the remaining tablespoon of oil over the hot grill or the broiler rack. Place the salmon on top and brush it with a few spoonfuls of the reserved marinade. Broil 3 or 4 inches from the heat, basting the salmon frequently with the remaining marinade. The salmon should be broiled for about 15 minutes on each side, or until it is evenly and delicately browned and feels firm when prodded gently with a finger.

Serve the salmon at once from a heated platter, with the lemon slices arranged attractively in a row along the top of the fish. Garnish it further, if you like, with red and green pepper strips and onion rings.

Planked Shad with Potatoes Duchesse

To serve 6

9 medium-sized boiling potatoes
   (about 3 pounds), peeled and
   quartered
Salt
3 egg yolks, lightly beaten
12 tablespoons butter, melted

½ teaspoon ground white pepper
A 2½- to 3-pound shad fillet, with
   the skin left on
2 tablespoons vegetable oil
Fresh parsley sprigs
2 lemons, each cut lengthwise into
   6 or 8 wedges

Drop the potatoes into enough lightly salted boiling water to cover them by at least 1 inch. Boil briskly, uncovered, until a potato quarter is soft enough to be easily mashed against the sides of the pan with the back of a spoon. Drain the potatoes in a sieve or colander, and pat them dry with paper towels.

Purée the potatoes through a food mill or ricer set into a deep bowl or place them in the bowl and mash them to a smooth purée with the back of a fork. Beat in the egg yolks and, when they are completely incorporated, add 6 tablespoons of the melted butter, 1½ teaspoons of salt and ½ teaspoon of white pepper. Cover the bowl tightly with foil to keep the purée warm.

Meanwhile, set the broiler pan and its rack 4 inches from the heat and preheat the broiler to its highest point. Wash the shad briefly under cold running water and pat it completely dry with paper towels. With a pastry brush, spread the vegetable oil evenly over the broiler pan rack and place the fish on top of it, skin side down. Brush the shad with 2 tablespoons of the remaining melted butter and broil about 4 inches from the heat for 6 to 8 minutes, basting the fish once or twice with 2 more tablespoons of the butter. The shad is done when its flesh is delicately browned and flakes easily when prodded gently with a table fork.

With the aid of two large metal spatulas, carefully transfer the shad to the center of an oak plank large enough to hold it comfortably. Using a pastry bag fitted with a large star tip, pipe the potato purée around the shad. Brush the shad with the remaining 2 tablespoons of melted butter and place the plank under the broiler for 2 or 3 minutes to brown the potatoes lightly.

Garnish the planked shad with the parsley sprigs and serve at once. Present the lemon wedges separately in a small bowl.

Shad Roe on a Bed of Sorrel

To serve 4

	A pinch of sugar
1 pound fresh sorrel	Salt
10 tablespoons unsalted butter, cut	Freshly ground black pepper
into ¼-inch bits	2 pairs shad roe
3 egg yolks	½ cup flour
¼ cup heavy cream	1 lemon, cut into 4 wedges

Wash the sorrel under cold running water. With a sharp knife, trim away any blemished spots and cut off the white stems. Stack the leaves together a handful at a time, roll them into a tight cylinder and cut it crosswise into fine shreds. Drop the sorrel into enough lightly salted boiling water to cover it by at least 1 inch and boil briskly for 2 or 3 minutes, until the shreds have wilted. Drain the sorrel thoroughly in a sieve.

Melt 4 tablespoons of the butter bits over moderate heat in a heavy 8- to 10-inch skillet. When the foam subsides, add the sorrel and stir it about to coat the shreds evenly. Then reduce the heat to low. Beat the egg yolks and cream together with a wire whisk and pour the mixture slowly over the sorrel, stirring continuously. Add the sugar, 1 teaspoon of salt and a liberal grinding of pepper and stir for 1 to 2 minutes. Do not let the mixture come anywhere near a boil or the egg yolks will curdle. Remove the pan from the heat and cover to keep the sorrel warm.

With scissors or a small sharp knife, slit the membrane connecting each pair of roe. Sprinkle the roe with salt and a few grindings of pepper, dip them in the flour to coat both sides and shake off the excess. Melt the remaining 6 tablespoons of butter in a heavy 8- to 10-inch skillet. When the foam subsides, add the roe and fry them for 5 to 6 minutes on each side, regulating the heat so that they brown evenly without burning.

Spoon the sorrel onto 4 individual heated plates, dividing it evenly among them, and place the roe on top of each portion. Garnish with lemon and serve at once, accompanied if you like by boiled potatoes.

Philadelphia Baked Clams

To serve 4

1 tablespoon butter, softened, plus
    4 tablespoons butter, cut into
    ½-inch bits
1 quart shucked small hard-shell
    clams *(see page 2)*
½ cup light cream
2 tablespoons dry sherry
½ teaspoon finely grated fresh

    lemon peel
¼ teaspoon anchovy paste
⅛ teaspoon crumbled dried thyme
4 drops Tabasco sauce
½ cup fresh crumbs made from
    saltine crackers, placed between
    sheets of wax paper and coarsely
    crushed with a rolling pin

Preheat the oven to 450°. With a pastry brush, spread the tablespoon of softened butter evenly over the bottom and sides of an 8- to 9-inch shallow baking dish.

Spread the clams on paper towels and pat them completely dry with more paper towels. Then arrange them in one or two layers in the buttered dish. Combine the cream, the 4 tablespoons of butter bits, the sherry, lemon peel, anchovy paste, thyme and Tabasco in a small saucepan. Stirring constantly, cook over moderate heat until the butter melts.

Pour the cream mixture over the clams and sprinkle the cracker crumbs on top. Bake in the middle of the oven for 10 minutes, or until the top is brown and the sauce bubbles. Serve at once from the baking dish.

New York Oyster Stew

To serve 4

4 tablespoons plus 4 teaspoons
    butter
2 teaspoons Worcestershire sauce
1 teaspoon paprika
½ teaspoon celery salt

1 teaspoon salt
2 dozen oysters, shucked and
    drained, with 1 cup of their
    liquor strained and reserved
½ cup light cream
½ cup milk

In a heavy 2- to 3-quart saucepan, melt 4 tablespoons of the butter over moderate heat and stir in the Worcestershire, paprika, celery salt and salt. Add the oysters and oyster liquor and bring to a boil over high heat. Reduce the heat to low and stir in the cream and milk. Stirring gently, cook for 2 or 3 minutes longer, until the oysters plump up and their edges begin to curl. Taste for seasoning.

Place a teaspoon of the remaining butter in each of four heated soup plates, ladle in the oyster stew and serve at once. Traditionally the stew is accompanied by oyster crackers.

Steamer Clams Remoulade

To serve 4 to 6 as a first course

4 dozen small soft-shell, or long-
neck, steamer clams *(see page
2)*, about 3 pounds
3 or 4 fresh parsley sprigs
2 tablespoons coarsely chopped
celery leaves
3 cups water
1½ cups freshly made mayonnaise

(page 7), or substitute 1½
cups unsweetened bottled
mayonnaise
2 tablespoons finely grated onion
2 tablespoons finely chopped fresh
parsley
2 tablespoons strained fresh lemon
juice
1 tablespoon prepared mustard

Wash the clams thoroughly under cold running water, discarding any with broken shells as well as those whose necks do not retract when prodded gently with a finger.

Combine the parsley sprigs, celery leaves and water in an 8- to 10-quart steamer or casserole and bring to a boil over high heat. Add the clams, cover tightly, and steam for 5 to 8 minutes, turning the clams about in the pot once or twice with a slotted spoon. All the shells should open; discard any clams that remain shut.

Transfer the clams to a plate. Strain the clam broth through a fine sieve and reserve it for consommé Bellevue *(page 12)* or another use. Remove the clams from their shells and cut off and discard the long black necks, or siphons. Wash the clams briefly in a sieve or colander set under cold running water, spread them on paper towels to drain, and pat them completely dry with fresh towels.

In a deep bowl, stir the mayonnaise, onion, chopped parsley, lemon juice and mustard together. When they are well blended, add the clams, and turn them about with a spoon to coat them evenly with the remoulade. Cover the bowl with plastic wrap or foil and refrigerate for 1 hour before serving.

If you like, you may shape the chilled lettuce leaves into cups on individual serving plates and spoon the clams remoulade into the cups in equal portions.

Oysters Casino

To serve 4

Rock salt	1 teaspoon Worcestershire sauce
2 slices lean bacon	3 drops Tabasco sauce
½ cup finely chopped shallots	2 dozen large oysters, shucked, and
¼ cup finely chopped celery	the deeper half shell of each
2 tablespoons finely chopped green	reserved
pepper	1 lemon, cut lengthwise into
2 teaspoons strained fresh lemon	quarters
juice	

Preheat the broiler to its highest setting. Spread the rock salt to a depth of about ½ inch in 6 individual shallow baking pans—each large enough to hold half a dozen oysters comfortably. (Or spread a ½-inch layer of salt in the bottom of one or two shallow baking-serving dishes that are large enough to hold all of the oysters.) Arrange the pans on one or two large baking sheets and set them in the oven to heat the salt while you prepare the oysters.

In a heavy 6- to 8-inch skillet, fry the bacon over moderate heat until it is crisp and brown and has rendered all its fat. With a slotted spoon, transfer the bacon to paper towels to drain. Crumble the bacon and set aside.

Add the shallots, celery and green pepper to the fat remaining in the skillet and, stirring frequently, cook for about 5 minutes, or until the vegetables are soft but not brown. Drain the vegetables in a small sieve and drop them into a bowl. Add the reserved bacon, the lemon juice, Worcestershire and Tabasco, and toss together gently but thoroughly.

Scrub the oyster shells thoroughly under cold running water, then pat them dry. Arrange them in a single layer in the salt-lined pans and place an oyster in each shell.

Spoon the vegetable-and-bacon mixture on top of the oysters, dividing it evenly among them.

Broil about 3 inches from the heat for 4 to 5 minutes, or until the oysters plump up and their edges begin to curl slightly. Serve at once, directly from the baking dishes, and garnish the oysters with lemon wedges.

NOTE: While the bed of salt helps to keep the shells from tipping and, if heated beforehand, will keep the oysters hot, it is not indispensable to the success of this dish. You may, if you like, bake the oysters in any shallow baking pan or pans large enough to hold the shells snugly in one layer, and serve them from a heated platter.

John Clancy's Broiled Clams

To serve 6

½ pound butter, cut into ½-inch bits and softened
1 tablespoon finely chopped fresh parsley
1 teaspoon finely chopped garlic
1 teaspoon Worcestershire sauce
½ teaspoon crumbled dried oregano
½ teaspoon salt
¼ teaspoon freshly ground black pepper
Rock salt
3 dozen small hard-shell clams *(see page 2),* shucked, with the deeper half shell of each reserved
¾ cup soft fresh crumbs made from homemade-type white bread, pulverized in a blender or finely shredded with a fork

Cream the butter by beating and mashing it against the sides of a bowl with the back of a spoon until it is light and fluffy. Beat in the parsley, garlic, Worcestershire, oregano, salt and pepper. With your hands, pat and shape the butter mixture into a cylinder 9 to 10 inches long and 1 inch in diameter. Wrap in wax paper and refrigerate the cylinder for at least 2 hours, or until it is firm.

Preheat the broiler to its highest setting. Spread the rock salt to a depth of about ½ inch in six individual shallow baking pans—each large enough to hold half a dozen clams comfortably. (Or spread a ½-inch layer of salt in the bottom of one or two shallow baking-serving dishes large enough to hold all the clams.) Arrange the pans on one or two large baking sheets and set them in the oven to heat the salt while you prepare the clams.

Scrub the reserved clam shells thoroughly under cold running water, then pat them dry and place a clam in each shell. With a small sharp knife, cut the cylinder of butter into ¼-inch-thick slices. Sprinkle each clam with 1 teaspoon of the bread crumbs and set a slice of seasoned butter on top. Then arrange the clams in one layer in the salt-lined pans.

Broil the clams about 4 inches from the heat for 3 minutes, or until the crumb topping is brown. Serve at once, directly from the baking dishes.

NOTE: The bed of salt is not indispensable to the success of this dish, but it will help keep the shells from tipping and, if heated beforehand, will keep the clams hot. You may, if you like, bake the clams in any shallow pan or pans large enough to hold the shells snugly in one layer, and serve them from a heated platter.

Clam Fritters

To make about 20 two-inch round
fritters

2 cups shucked soft-shell, or long-
neck, clams *(see page 2)*
2 egg yolks
1 cup fine crumbs made from saltine
crackers, pulverized in a blender
or placed between sheets of wax
paper and crushed with a rolling
pin

A pinch of ground hot red pepper
(cayenne)
1 teaspoon salt
⅛ teaspoon freshly ground black
pepper
4 egg whites
Vegetable oil

Drain the clams and discard all but 4 teaspoons of the clam liquor. With a sharp knife, cut off the dark necks of the clams and discard them; chop the soft round bodies of the clams coarsely.

In a deep bowl, beat the egg yolks lightly with a wire whisk or fork. Add the chopped clams, clam liquor, cracker crumbs, red pepper, salt and black pepper and stir together thoroughly.

In a separate bowl, beat the egg whites with a whisk or a rotary or electric beater until they are stiff enough to form unwavering peaks on the beater when it is lifted from the bowl. With a rubber spatula, scoop the egg whites over the clam mixture and fold them together gently.

Preheat the oven to its lowest setting. Line a large shallow baking dish with paper towels and place it in the center of the oven.

Pour the oil into a heavy 10- to 12-inch skillet to a depth of about ½ inch, and heat until it is very hot but not smoking. To make each fritter, pour 1 tablespoon of the batter into the hot oil. Leaving enough space so that they can spread into 2-inch cakes, fry the fritters 5 or 6 at a time for about 3 minutes on each side. When they are brown and crisp around the edges, transfer the fritters to the lined pan and keep them warm in the oven while you fry the rest.

Serve the fritters as soon as they are all cooked, accompanied if you wish by lemon wedges.

Clam Tart

To make one 9-inch tart

4 dozen small soft-shell, or long-
    neck, steamer clams *(see page
    2)*
4 eggs
1 cup light cream
¼ teaspoon ground nutmeg,
    preferably freshly grated
½ teaspoon salt
⅛ teaspoon ground white pepper
4 slices lean bacon
2 tablespoons finely chopped onion
A 9-inch short-crust nonsweet pastry
    shell, partially baked *(page 6)*

Preheat the oven to 375°. Wash the clams thoroughly under cold running water and discard any with broken shells as well as those whose necks do not retract when prodded gently with a finger. With a small sharp knife shuck the clams over a bowl, then strain the clam liquor through a fine sieve lined with a double thickness of cheesecloth and reserve ½ cup of it. Cut the soft centers out of the clams, discarding the long black necks, or siphons, and the tough muscles that hold the clams to their shells. Chop the clam meat fine.

Beat the eggs lightly with a wire whisk or a rotary or electric beater. Add the ½ cup of strained clam liquor, the cream, nutmeg, salt and pepper, and continue to beat until the custard mixture is smooth. Stir in the chopped clams.

In a heavy 10- to 12-inch skillet fry the bacon over moderate heat, turning the slices frequently with kitchen tongs until they are crisp and brown and have rendered all their fat. Drain the bacon slices on paper towels and crumble them into bits.

Pour off all but a thin film of fat from the skillet and add the onion. Stirring frequently, cook for about 5 minutes, until they are soft and translucent but not brown. With a rubber spatula, scrape the contents of the skillet into the custard. Add the bacon bits and mix well.

Pour the custard mixture into the partially baked pie shell and bake in the upper third of the oven for about 25 minutes, or until a knife inserted in the center comes out clean. Serve the clam tart hot or warm.

Broiled Skewered Scallops

To serve 4

1 pound (1 pint) fresh or defrosted
   frozen bay scallops
2 tablespoons strained fresh lemon
   juice
1 teaspoon salt
¼ teaspoon freshly ground black

pepper
8 slices lean bacon
8 tablespoons butter, melted and
   cooled
1 lemon, cut lengthwise into
   quarters

Light a layer of briquettes in a charcoal broiler and let them burn until a white ash begins to appear on the surface, or preheat your kitchen broiler to its highest setting.

Wash the scallops under cold running water, spread them on paper towels, and pat them completely dry with fresh towels. Combine the lemon juice, salt and pepper in a small bowl and mix well. Drop in the scallops and turn them about with a spoon to coat them evenly.

Thread the scallops and bacon onto four long skewers, looping the bacon slices up and down to weave them over and under alternate scallops. Push the scallops compactly together. With a pastry brush, thoroughly coat the scallops with a few spoonfuls of the melted butter.

Broil about 4 inches from the heat, turning the skewers from time to time and basting the scallops frequently with the remaining melted butter. They should broil for about 4 to 5 minutes. The scallops are done when they are opaque and firm to the touch, and the bacon is brown.

With the side of a knife, slide the scallops and bacon off the skewers onto a heated platter. Serve at once, accompanied by the lemon quarters.

Broiled Bluefish Fillets

To serve 4

4 eight-ounce bluefish fillets, with
   skin left on
2 tablespoons strained fresh lemon
   juice

1 teaspoon salt
1 tablespoon vegetable oil
4 tablespoons butter, melted
¼ cup sesame seeds

Set the broiler pan and its grid 4 inches from the heat and preheat the broiler to its highest point. Wash the fillets briefly under cold running water and pat them completely dry with paper towels. Season the fish on both sides with the lemon juice and salt.

With a pastry brush, spread the vegetable oil over the grid of the broiler pan and arrange the bluefish fillets on it, skin side down. Brush the fillets with 2 tablespoons of the melted butter and broil about 4 inches from the heat for 4 to 5 minutes. Baste the fish once or twice with the remaining butter. The fillets are done when the flesh is lightly brown and flakes easily if prodded gently with a fork.

Sprinkle the sesame seeds evenly over the fillets and broil for a minute or so longer to brown the seeds. Serve at once.

Lobster Croquettes

To serve 4

2 tablespoons butter
2 tablespoons flour
½ cup milk
1 egg, lightly beaten
1 teaspoon Worcestershire sauce
¼ teaspoon Tabasco sauce
¼ teaspoon salt
1 pound freshly cooked, frozen or
  canned lobster meat, drained
  thoroughly, picked over to

remove all bits of shell and
  cartilage and coarsely chopped
  (about 2 cups)
1 cup fresh crumbs made from
  unsalted soda crackers, pulverized
  in a blender or placed between 2
  pieces of wax paper and finely
  crushed with a rolling pin
Vegetable oil for deep frying
Tartar sauce *(page 63)*

In a heavy 1- to 2-quart saucepan, melt the butter over moderate heat. When the foam begins to subside, add the flour and mix well. Stirring the mixture constantly with a wire whisk, pour in the milk in a slow, thin stream and cook over moderate heat until the sauce comes to a boil, thickens and is smooth. Reduce the heat to low and simmer for 2 or 3 minutes to remove any taste of raw flour.

Stir a tablespoonful of the simmering sauce into the beaten egg. Whisking constantly, pour the mixture into the pan and, when the sauce is smooth, add the Worcestershire, Tabasco and salt. Taste for seasoning, remove the pan from the heat, and stir in the lobster meat. Refrigerate for about 1 hour, or until the mixture is firm.

Divide the lobster mixture into 4 equal portions and, with your hands, pat and shape each one into a cork-shaped croquette about 2 inches in diameter and 2½ inches long. Roll the croquettes in the cracker crumbs to coat all sides evenly, then place them on wax paper and refrigerate until ready to fry.

Pour vegetable oil into a deep fryer or large heavy saucepan to a depth of 3 inches and heat the oil until it reaches a temperature of 375° on a deep-frying thermometer. Fry the croquettes for 2 or 3 minutes, turning them with a slotted spoon until they are golden brown on all sides.

Drain the croquettes briefly on paper towels, then arrange them on a heated platter and serve at once, accompanied by a bowl of tartar sauce.

Lobster Thermidor

To serve 4

4 live 1½-pound lobsters
3 tablespoons butter, plus
    4 teaspoons butter cut into
    ¼-inch bits
1 cup finely chopped fresh
    mushrooms
¼ cup brandy
2 cups heavy cream
6 egg yolks, lightly beaten
1 tablespoon Worcestershire sauce
1 tablespoon finely chopped
    pimiento

1 tablespoon finely chopped fresh
    parsley
¼ teaspoon ground hot red pepper
    (cayenne)
2 drops Tabasco sauce
1½ teaspoons salt
¼ cup freshly grated imported
    Parmesan cheese
¼ cup soft fresh crumbs made
    from homemade-type white
    bread, pulverized in a blender or
    finely shredded with a fork

Pour enough water into a 12- to 14-quart pot to fill it halfway, and bring the water to a boil over high heat. Plunge two of the lobsters headfirst into the pot. Both the lobsters should be entirely submerged; if not, add more boiling water.

Cover the pot tightly, return the water to a boil, then reduce the heat to moderate and boil the lobsters for 15 minutes. Regulate the heat if necessary to prevent the water from boiling over, but keep the liquid at a boil throughout the cooking.

To test for doneness, remove one lobster from the pot. Grasp the end of one of the small legs at either side of the body and jerk it sharply. If the leg pulls away from the body, the lobster is done. If the leg remains attached to the body, boil the lobsters for 2 or 3 minutes longer.

With tongs or a slotted spoon, transfer the cooked lobsters to a platter to drain, and boil the remaining 2 lobsters in the same water, adding more water if necessary.

One at a time place the boiled lobsters on a cutting board. Twist off the large claws at the point where they meet the body, crack each claw in two or three places with a cleaver, and pick out all the meat. Cut the lobster meat into ½-inch pieces and reserve it; discard the claw shells.

Twist off the antennae and the legs and discard them. Turn the lobster on its back and, with kitchen scissors, cut lengthwise through the soft tail and stomach shell. Remove and discard the gelatinous sac (stomach) in the head and the long white intestinal vein attached to it. Scoop out and save the greenish-brown tomalley (liver) and the red coral (roe) if any. Lift the tail meat out in one piece and cut it into ½-inch cubes. Set the lobster meat and body shell aside and prepare the three remaining lobsters in the same manner.

About half an hour before you plan to serve the lobsters, preheat the oven to 350°. In a heavy 10- to 12-inch skillet, melt 3 tablespoons of butter over moderate heat. When the foam begins to subside, add the mushrooms and, stirring occasionally, cook uncovered for 8 to 10 minutes, or until the liquid that accumulates in the pan has evaporated. Do not let the mushrooms brown. Stir in the reserved lobster meat.

Warm the brandy in a small saucepan over low heat, ignite it with a match, and pour it flaming over the lobster mixture a little at a time, sliding the skillet gently back and forth until the flames die. Stir in the cream and cook over moderate heat until it comes to a boil.

Reduce the heat to its lowest setting. Ladle about 2 tablespoons of the hot cream into the egg yolks, mix well, and pour the mixture into the skillet. Stirring constantly, simmer over low heat for 2 or 3 minutes, until the sauce thickens and is smooth. Do not let the sauce come anywhere near a boil or the egg yolks will curdle.

Remove the skillet from the heat and stir in the Worcestershire, pimiento, parsley, red pepper, Tabasco and salt. Taste for seasoning. Spoon the lobster-and-mushroom mixture and the sauce into the reserved shells, dividing the mixture evenly among them. Mix together the grated cheese and bread crumbs, and sprinkle them over the lobsters. Dot the tops with the 4 teaspoons of butter bits.

Arrange the lobsters side by side on one or two large baking sheets and bake in the middle of the oven for about 15 minutes, or until the sauce has begun to bubble and the crumb topping has become golden brown. Serve at once.

NOTE: After the lobsters are boiled, the lobster meat and body shells may be separately covered with foil or plastic wrap and safely kept in the refrigerator for up to 24 hours. Or, if you prefer, lobster thermidor may be completely assembled ready for baking, then tightly wrapped and refrigerated for up to 24 hours.

BREADS, BISCUITS & BREAKFAST CAKES

Sour-Cream Cornbread

To serve 4 to 6

1 tablespoon butter, softened, plus
   1 tablespoon butter, cut into
   ¼-inch bits and softened
1 cup cornmeal
1 cup unsifted flour
2 tablespoons sugar

1 teaspoon baking soda
1 teaspoon cream of tartar
1 teaspoon salt
1 egg, lightly beaten
1 cup sour cream
¼ cup milk

Preheat the oven to 425°. With a pastry brush, spread 1 tablespoon of softened butter evenly over the bottom and sides of an 8-by-8-by-2-inch baking dish. Set aside.

Combine the cornmeal, flour, sugar, baking soda, cream of tartar and salt, and sift them together into a deep mixing bowl. With a large wooden spoon, beat in the egg and, when it is completely incorporated, add the sour cream, milk and the tablespoon of butter bits.

With a rubber spatula, scrape the entire contents of the bowl into the buttered baking dish. Spread the cornbread mixture to the edges of the dish and smooth the top with the spatula. Bake in the middle of the oven for 20 minutes, or until the top is golden brown and a cake tester or toothpick inserted in the center comes out clean.

Serve the sour-cream cornbread at once, directly from the baking dish.

Wild-Persimmon and Hickory-Nut Bread

To make two 9-by-5-by-3-inch
  loaves

14 tablespoons butter, softened
4 tablespoons plus 2 cups unsifted
  flour
1 teaspoon baking soda
½ teaspoon salt

1 pound fully ripe wild persimmons
  (about 2 dozen)
1 cup sugar
2 eggs
1 cup coarsely chopped hickory nuts

Preheat the oven to 325°. With a pastry brush, spread 2 tablespoons of the softened butter over the bottom and sides of two 9-by-5-by-3-inch loaf pans. Add 2 tablespoons of the flour to each pan, tipping the pan back and forth to distribute the flour evenly. Invert the pans and rap them sharply on the bottoms to remove the excess flour.

Combine the 2 cups of flour, the baking soda and salt, and sift them together onto a plate or sheet of wax paper. Set aside.

Wash the persimmons gently under cold running water and let them drain in a colander. With a small sharp knife, cut them into quarters and pick out the seeds. Purée the persimmons through a food mill set over a bowl, or rub them through a coarse sieve with the back of a spoon. You will need about 1 cup of puréed fruit.

In a deep bowl, cream the remaining 12 tablespoons of softened butter and the sugar by beating and mashing them against the sides of the bowl with the back of a spoon until light and fluffy. Beat in the eggs, one at a time. Add 1 cup of the flour mixture and, when it is thoroughly incorporated, beat in about ½ cup of the puréed fruit. Add the remaining 1 cup of the flour mixture and then the rest of the purée, beating well after each addition. Stir in the hickory nuts.

Pour the batter into the two buttered-and-floured pans, dividing it equally between them and spreading it evenly with a rubber spatula. Bake in the middle of the oven for about 1 hour, or until the loaves begin to shrink away from the sides of the pans and a toothpick or cake tester inserted in the centers comes out clean.

Turn the loaves out on wire racks to cool. Serve the bread warm or at room temperature.

Dilly Bread

To make one 9-by-5-by-3-inch loaf

¼ cup lukewarm water (110° to 115°)
1 package active dry yeast
1 teaspoon plus 2 tablespoons sugar
1 tablespoon butter, cut into ¼-inch bits, plus 3 tablespoons butter, softened
2 tablespoons finely chopped onions
2 to 2½ cups unsifted flour

¼ teaspoon baking soda
1 teaspoon salt
1 cup large-curd cottage cheese (8 ounces)
1 egg
2 teaspoons dill seed
1 egg lightly beaten with 1 tablespoon milk
Coarse (kosher) salt

Pour the lukewarm water into a small bowl and add the yeast and 1 teaspoon of the sugar. Let the yeast and sugar rest for 2 or 3 minutes, then mix well. Set in a warm, draft-free place (such as an unlighted oven) for about 10 minutes, or until the yeast bubbles up and the mixture almost doubles in volume.

Meanwhile, melt the tablespoon of butter bits over moderate heat in a small skillet. When the foam begins to subside, add the onions and, stirring frequently, cook for 2 or 3 minutes, until they are soft but not brown. Set aside.

Combine 2 cups of the flour, the remaining 2 tablespoons of sugar, the baking soda and salt, and sift them together into a deep mixing bowl. Make a well in the center and scrape in the entire contents of the skillet. Add the yeast mixture, the cottage cheese, egg and dill seed, and gradually incorporate the dry ingredients into the liquid ones with a large wooden spoon. Continue to stir until the dough is smooth and can be gathered into a medium-soft ball.

Place the ball on a lightly floured surface and knead, pushing the dough down with the heels of your hands, pressing it forward and folding it back on itself. As you knead, sprinkle flour over the ball by the tablespoonful, adding up to ½ cup more flour if necessary to make a firm dough. Knead for about 10 minutes longer, until the dough is smooth, shiny and elastic.

With a pastry brush, spread 1 tablespoon of the softened butter evenly over the inside of a large bowl. Set the ball of dough in the bowl and turn it about to butter the entire surface. Drape the bowl loosely with a kitchen towel and set it aside in the draft-free place for about 1 hour, or until it has doubled in volume.

Brush 1 tablespoon of the remaining softened butter over the bottom and sides of a 9-by-5-by-3-inch loaf pan. Punch the dough down with a blow of your fist and, on a lightly floured surface, shape it into a loaf about 8 inches long and 4 inches wide. Place the dough in the buttered pan and set it in the draft-free place to rise again for about 45 minutes.

Preheat the oven to 375°. (If you have used the oven to let the bread rise, gently transfer the loaf to another warm place to rest while the oven heats.) Brush the top of the bread with the egg-and-milk mixture, then bake in the middle of the oven for 30 to 35 minutes, or until the loaf is golden brown. To test for doneness, turn the loaf out on a flat surface and rap the bottom sharply with your knuckles. The loaf should sound hollow; if not, put it back in the pan and bake for 5 to 10 minutes longer.

Place the bread on a wire rack and brush the top with the remaining tablespoon of softened butter. Sprinkle lightly with coarse salt and let the bread cool before serving.

Potato Bread, Shaker Style

To make two 9-by-5-by-3-inch
   loaves

2 cups water
2 medium-sized boiling potatoes,
   peeled and quartered
1 package active dry yeast
1 teaspoon plus ½ cup sugar
5½ to 6½ cups unsifted flour

½ teaspoon salt
2 eggs
8 tablespoons butter, cut into
   ½-inch bits and softened, plus
   3 tablespoons butter, softened
1 egg lightly beaten with
   1 tablespoon milk

Bring the water to a boil in a small heavy saucepan. Drop in the potatoes and boil briskly, uncovered, until a piece of potato can be easily mashed against the side of the pan with the back of a fork. Drain the potatoes in a sieve set over a bowl and pat them dry with paper towels. (Measure and reserve 1 cup of potato water.) Purée the potatoes through a food mill set over a bowl, or mash them with the back of a fork. You will need 1 cup of purée.

When the potato water has cooled to lukewarm (110° to 115°), pour ¼ cup of it into a shallow bowl. Add the yeast and 1 teaspoon of the sugar. Let the mixture stand for 2 or 3 minutes, then stir well. Set the bowl in a warm, draft-free place (such as an unlighted oven) for 5 minutes, until the yeast bubbles and the mixture almost doubles in bulk.

Combine 5½ cups of the flour, the remaining ½ cup of sugar and the salt in a deep mixing bowl and make a well in the center. Add the

Continued on next page

cup of potato purée, the yeast mixture, eggs, the remaining ¾ cup of potato water and the 8 tablespoons of butter bits. With a large spoon, mix the ingredients together and stir until the dough is smooth and can be gathered into a soft ball.

Place the ball on a lightly floured surface and knead, pushing the dough down with the heels of your hands, pressing it forward and folding it back on itself. As you knead, sprinkle flour over the ball by the tablespoonful, adding up to 1 cup more flour if necessary to make a firm dough. Continue to knead for about 10 minutes, or until the dough is smooth, shiny and elastic.

With a pastry brush, spread 1 tablespoon of the softened butter evenly inside a deep mixing bowl. Place the ball in the bowl and turn it around to butter the entire surface of the dough. Drape the bowl loosely with a kitchen towel and put it in the warm place for about 1½ hours, or until the dough doubles in volume.

Brush the remaining 2 tablespoons of softened butter evenly over the bottoms and sides of two 9-by-5-by-3-inch loaf pans. Punch the dough down with a blow of your fist and divide it in half. Pat and shape each half into a loaf about 8 inches long and 4 inches wide. Place the dough in the buttered pans and set aside in the warm place to rise again for about 45 minutes, or until doubled in bulk.

Preheat the oven to 375°. (If you have used the oven to let the loaves rise, gently transfer the pans to another warm place to rest while the oven heats.) Brush the tops with the beaten egg-and-milk mixture and bake the loaves in the middle of the oven for about 35 minutes, or until they are golden brown. To test for doneness, turn the loaves out on a flat surface and rap the bottoms sharply with your knuckles. The loaves should sound hollow; if they don't, return them to their pans and bake for 5 to 10 minutes longer.

Turn the potato bread out on wire racks and let it cool before serving.

Cornmeal Griddle Cakes

To make about 1 dozen 4-inch
    pancakes

1 cup cornmeal
1 cup unsifted flour
1 teaspoon double-acting baking
    powder
½ teaspoon salt
2 cups buttermilk
3 egg yolks, lightly beaten
6 tablespoons butter, melted and
    cooled
3 egg whites

Combine the cornmeal, flour, baking powder and salt, and sift them together into a deep bowl. Stir in the buttermilk with a wooden spoon and,
when it is completely incorporated, add the egg yolks and 2 tablespoons
of the melted, cooled butter.

With a wire whisk or a rotary or electric beater, beat the egg whites in
a separate bowl until they are stiff enough to stand in unwavering peaks
on the beater when it is lifted from the bowl. Scoop the egg whites over
the cornmeal mixture and, with a rubber spatula, fold them together
gently but thoroughly.

Warm a large heavy griddle over moderate heat until a drop of water
flicked onto it splutters and evaporates instantly. Grease the griddle lightly
with a pastry brush dipped in the remaining 4 tablespoons of butter.
To form each griddle cake, pour ¼ cup of the batter on the griddle, leaving enough space between them so that they can spread into 4-inch rounds.
Fry 3 or 4 cakes at a time for about 3 minutes on each side, or until they
are golden and crisp around the edges.

As they brown, arrange the griddle cakes on a heated plate. Then repeat the procedure, brushing the griddle with melted butter when necessary, until all the cakes are fried. Serve the cornmeal griddle cakes at
once with butter and maple syrup.

Salt-rising Bread

To make two 9-by-5-by-3-inch
   loaves

½ cup stone-ground cornmeal	1 tablespoon salt
4 cups milk	9 to 9½ cups unsifted flour
5 tablespoons vegetable shortening,	2 tablespoons butter, softened
cut into ¼-inch bits	1 egg lightly beaten with
1 tablespoon sugar	1 tablespoon milk

Starting a day ahead, measure the cornmeal into a heatproof bowl. Then heat 1 cup of the milk in a small saucepan until bubbles begin to form around the sides of the pan. Pour the milk over the cornmeal and stir to a smooth paste. Set the bowl in a warm draft-free place (such as an unlighted oven) overnight, or until the cornmeal mixture ferments and develops a strong cheeselike odor.

Place the bits of shortening, the sugar and salt in a mixing bowl 12 inches in diameter across the top. At the same time, pour water to a depth of 2 or 3 inches into a pot or saucepan 12 inches in diameter. The rim of the bowl should fit snugly over the rim of the pot; the pot must be deep enough so that the bottom of the bowl will be suspended above the water. Bring the water to a boil over high heat, then remove the pot from the stove and cover tightly to keep the water hot.

In a heavy 1- to 2-quart saucepan, heat the remaining 3 cups of milk until bubbles form around the sides of the pan. Pour the milk over the shortening and stir until the sugar and salt dissolve. Add 3½ cups of the flour and, when it is incorporated, stir in the cornmeal mixture.

Set the bowl over the pot of water and drape the top with a kitchen towel. Let the dough rise for about 2 hours, or until bubbles form on its surface. The water under the bowl must be kept at least lukewarm; check the pot occasionally and replenish with boiling water if necessary.

When the dough has fermented, remove the bowl from the pot. Stir in up to 6 cups more flour, 1 cup at a time, to make a firm ball. If the dough becomes difficult to stir, work in the remaining flour with your hands.

Place the dough on a lightly floured surface and knead it by pressing the dough down with the heels of your hands, pushing it forward and folding it back on itself. Repeat for about 20 minutes, until the dough is smooth and elastic.

With a pastry brush, spread the softened butter evenly over the bottom and sides of two 9-by-5-by-3-inch loaf pans. Divide the dough in half and shape each piece into a loaf about 8 inches long and 4 inches wide. Place the loaves in the buttered pans and set them aside in the draft-free place for 2 hours, or until the dough rises and the loaves double in bulk.

Preheat the oven to 400°. (If you have used the oven to let the bread rise, gently transfer the loaves to another warm place to rest while the oven heats.) Brush the tops of the loaves with the egg-and-milk mixture and bake in the middle of the oven for 10 minutes. Reduce the oven temperature to 350° and continue baking for 25 to 30 minutes longer, or until the bread is golden brown. To test for doneness, turn the loaves out on a flat surface and rap the bottoms sharply with your knuckles. The loaves should sound hollow; if not, slide them back into the pans and bake for 5 to 10 minutes more.

Place the bread on wire racks and let it cool before serving.

Whole-Wheat Bread

To make one 9-by-5-by-3-inch loaf

½ cup lukewarm water (110° to 115°)

1 package active dry yeast

1 teaspoon sugar

¼ cup dark molasses

½ cup lukewarm milk (110° to 115°)

2 to 2½ cups whole-wheat flour

1 cup unsifted all-purpose flour

1 teaspoon salt

4 tablespoons butter, cut into ½-inch bits and softened, plus 2 tablespoons butter, softened

1 egg lightly beaten with 1 tablespoon milk

Pour the lukewarm water into a small bowl and sprinkle in the yeast and sugar. Let the yeast and sugar rest for 2 or 3 minutes, then mix well. Set the bowl in a warm, draft-free place (such as an unlighted oven) for about 10 minutes, or until the yeast bubbles up and the mixture almost doubles in volume.

Pour the molasses into the milk and stir until well blended. Then place 2 cups of whole-wheat flour, the cup of all-purpose flour and the salt in a deep mixing bowl and make a well in the center. Pour in the yeast and the molasses-and-milk mixtures and, with a large wooden spoon, gradually incorporate the dry ingredients into the liquid ones. Stir until the mixture is smooth, then beat in the 4 tablespoons of butter bits, a few teaspoonfuls at a time. Continue to beat until the dough can be gathered into a medium-soft ball.

Place the ball on a lightly floured surface and knead, pushing the dough down with the heels of your hands, pressing it forward and fold-

Continued on next page

ing it back on itself. As you knead, sprinkle whole-wheat flour over the ball by the tablespoonful, adding up to ½ cup flour if necessary to make a firm dough. Knead for about 10 minutes longer, until the dough is smooth and elastic.

With a pastry brush, spread 1 tablespoon of the softened butter evenly over the inside of a large bowl. Set the dough in the bowl and turn it about to butter the entire surface. Drape the bowl with a kitchen towel and set it aside in the draft-free place for 1 to 1½ hours, or until the dough doubles in volume.

Brush the remaining tablespoon of softened butter over the bottom and sides of a 9-by-5-by-3-inch loaf pan. Punch the dough down with a blow of your fist and, on a lightly floured surface, shape it into a loaf about 8 inches long and 4 inches wide. Place the dough in the buttered pan and set it in the draft-free place to rise again for about 45 minutes.

Preheat the oven to 450°. (If you have used the oven to let the bread rise, gently transfer the loaf to another warm place to rest while the oven heats.) Brush the top of the whole-wheat bread with the egg-and-milk mixture, then bake in the middle of the oven for 35 to 40 minutes, or until the loaf is golden brown. To test for doneness, turn the loaf out on a flat surface and rap the bottom sharply with your knuckles. The loaf should sound hollow; if not, slide it back into the pan and bake for 5 to 10 minutes longer.

Place the finished whole-wheat bread on a wire rack and let it cool before serving.

Pumpkin Bread

To make two 9-by-5-by-3-inch
loaves

10 tablespoons butter, softened
2 tablespoons plus 3 cups unsifted
flour
2 teaspoons baking soda
½ teaspoon double-acting baking
powder
1 teaspoon ground cinnamon
1 teaspoon ground cloves

1 teaspoon salt
2½ cups sugar
4 eggs
2 cups puréed pumpkin, freshly
cooked or canned
½ cup water
½ cup coarsely chopped walnuts
½ cup finely chopped seedless
raisins

Preheat the oven to 350°. With a pastry brush, spread 2 tablespoons of the softened butter over the bottom and sides of two 9-by-5-by-3-inch loaf pans. Sprinkle 1 tablespoon of the flour into each pan and tip it from side to side to spread the flour evenly. Invert the pans and rap the bottoms sharply to remove the excess flour.

Combine the remaining 3 cups of flour, the baking soda, baking powder, cinnamon, cloves and salt, and sift them together onto a plate or a sheet of wax paper. Set aside.

In a deep mixing bowl, cream the remaining 8 tablespoons of softened butter and the sugar together by beating and mashing them against the sides of the bowl with the back of a spoon until the mixture is light and fluffy. Beat in the eggs, one at a time, then stir in the pumpkin. Add about 1 cup of the flour mixture and, when it is completely incorporated, beat in 2 or 3 tablespoons of the water. Repeat two more times, alternating 1 cup of flour with 2 or 3 tablespoons of water, and beating well after each addition. Stir in the walnuts and raisins.

Ladle the batter into the two loaf pans, spreading it evenly and smoothing the tops with a rubber spatula. Bake in the middle of the oven for 50 to 60 minutes, or until the loaves shrink away from the sides of the pans and a cake tester or toothpick inserted in the centers comes out clean.

Turn the loaves of pumpkin bread out on wire cake racks and cool to room temperature before serving.

Fried Yeast Biscuits

To make about 1 dozen 2½-inch
   biscuits

¼ cup lukewarm water (110° to
   115°)
1 package active dry yeast
1 teaspoon plus 2 tablespoons sugar
3 to 3½ cups unsifted flour
1½ teaspoons salt

1 cup lukewarm milk (110° to
   115°)
4 tablespoons lard, cut into ¼-inch
   bits and softened
1 tablespoon butter, softened
Vegetable oil for deep frying

Pour the water into a small bowl and add the yeast and 1 teaspoon of the sugar. Let the yeast and sugar rest for 2 or 3 minutes, then mix well. Set in a warm, draft-free place (such as an unlighted oven) for 10 minutes, or until the yeast bubbles up and the mixture almost doubles in volume.

Place 3 cups of the flour, the remaining 2 tablespoons of sugar and the salt in a deep mixing bowl and make a well in the center. Pour in the yeast mixture and the milk and, with a large wooden spoon, gradually beat the dry ingredients into the liquid ones. Add the bits of lard and continue to beat until the dough is smooth and can be gathered into a compact ball.

Place the ball on a lightly floured surface and knead, pushing the dough down with the heels of your hands, pressing it forward and folding it back on itself. As you knead, incorporate up to ½ cup more flour by the tablespoonful, until the dough is no longer moist and sticky. Then continue to knead for about 10 minutes, or until the dough is smooth, shiny and elastic. Gather the dough into a ball.

With a pastry brush, spread the softened butter evenly over the inside of a large bowl. Set the ball of dough in the bowl and turn it about to butter the entire surface of the ball. Drape the bowl loosely with a kitchen towel and put it in the warm, draft-free place for about 1 hour to allow the dough to double in volume.

Pour vegetable oil into a deep fryer or large heavy saucepan to a depth of 2 to 3 inches and heat the oil until it reaches the temperature of 350° on a deep-frying thermometer.

Punch the dough down with a blow of your fist and, on a lightly floured surface, roll it out into a rough rectangle about ¾ inch thick. With a cookie cutter or the rim of a glass, cut the dough into 2½-inch rounds. Gather the scraps into a ball, roll them out as before, and cut out as many more 2½-inch rounds as you can.

Deep-fry the biscuits 3 or 4 at a time for about 5 minutes, turning them once with a slotted spatula so that they become puffed and brown on both sides. As they brown, transfer the biscuits to paper towels to drain briefly, then place them on a heated platter and drape foil over them to keep them warm while you fry the rest. Serve the biscuits hot.

Buttermilk Soda Biscuits

To make about 18 two-inch biscuits

1 tablespoon butter, softened, plus 4 tablespoons butter, melted and cooled
1¾ cups unsifted flour

1 tablespoon double-acting baking powder
½ teaspoon baking soda
1 teaspoon salt
¾ cup buttermilk

Preheat the oven to 450°. With a pastry brush, spread the tablespoon of softened butter evenly over a large baking sheet and set aside.

Combine the flour, baking powder, soda and salt, and sift them together into a deep bowl. Make a well in the center and pour in the cooled melted butter and the buttermilk. With a wooden spoon, gradually incorporate the dry ingredients into the liquid ones. Then stir until the dough is smooth, but do not beat or overmix or the biscuits will be heavy.

Gather the dough into a ball, place it on a lightly floured surface, and roll it out about ½ inch thick. With a biscuit cutter or the rim of a glass, cut the dough into 2-inch rounds. Gather the scraps together into a ball and roll out as before. Then cut as many more biscuits as you can.

Arrange the biscuits about 1 inch apart on the buttered baking sheet and bake in the middle of the oven for 10 to 12 minutes, or until the biscuits are golden brown. Serve at once.

Sugar Doughnuts

To make about 1½ dozen
doughnuts and 2 to 3 dozen
doughnut balls

4 to 5 cups unsifted flour
4 teaspoons double-acting baking
powder
¼ teaspoon ground nutmeg
½ teaspoon salt
¾ cup milk

4 tablespoons butter, melted and
cooled
1 teaspoon vanilla
3 eggs
1 cup granulated sugar
Vegetable oil for deep frying
2 cups confectioners' sugar, sifted

Combine 4 cups of the flour, the baking powder, nutmeg and salt, and sift them onto a plate or a sheet of wax paper. Pour the milk, cooled melted butter and vanilla into a measuring cup and mix well. Set aside.

In a deep bowl, beat the eggs and the granulated sugar with a wire whisk or a rotary or electric beater for 4 or 5 minutes, until the mixture falls in a slowly dissolving ribbon from the beater when it is lifted from the bowl. Add about 1 cup of the flour mixture and stir with a wooden spoon. When the flour is well incorporated, beat in about ¼ cup of the milk-and-butter mixture. Repeat three more times, alternating 1 cup of the flour with ¼ cup of the milk, and beating well after each addition. Add up to 1 cup more flour by the tablespoonful and continue to stir with the spoon, or knead with your hands, until the dough can be gathered into a compact ball. Cover the bowl with wax paper and refrigerate for at least 30 minutes.

Line two large baking sheets with wax paper. Cut off about one quarter of the dough and place it on a lightly floured surface. Flour a rolling pin and roll the dough out about ⅓ inch thick. If the dough sticks, dust a little flour over and under it.

With a 2¾-inch doughnut cutter, cut out as many doughnuts as you can. Using a wide metal spatula, transfer the doughnuts and their centers to the paper-lined pans. Refrigerate until ready to fry. Break off another quarter of the dough, roll it out, cut out more doughnuts and refrigerate as before. Repeat until all the dough has been used, but do not reroll the scraps or the doughnuts made from them may be tough. Instead use a 1-inch cutter to form balls out of the scraps.

Pour vegetable oil into a deep fryer or large heavy saucepan to a depth of 3 inches and heat the oil until it reaches a temperature of 375° on a deep-frying thermometer. Meanwhile place ½ cup of the confectioners' sugar in a paper bag and set it aside.

Deep-fry the doughnuts and balls 4 or 5 at a time, turning them about with a slotted spoon for 3 minutes, or until they are puffed and brown.

Drain the doughnuts briefly on paper towels, then drop 2 at a time into the paper bag and shake to coat them with sugar. (Add sugar to the bag as needed.) Place the doughnuts on wire racks to cool while you fry and sugar the rest.

Funnel Cakes

To make about 12 six-inch cakes

Vegetable oil for deep frying
2 cups unsifted flour
1 tablespoon sugar
1 teaspoon double-acting baking
   powder
¼ teaspoon salt
2 eggs, lightly beaten
1 to 1¼ cups milk

Preheat the oven to its lowest setting. Line two large baking sheets with paper towels and place them in the center of the oven. Pour vegetable oil into a heavy 12- to 14-inch skillet to a depth of about 1½ to 2 inches and heat the oil until it is very hot but not smoking.

Meanwhile, combine the flour, sugar, baking powder and salt and sift them together into a deep bowl. Make a well in the center and pour in the eggs and 1 cup of the milk. With a large spoon, gradually incorporate the dry ingredients into the liquid ones and stir until the batter is smooth.

To make the cakes, ladle ½ cup of batter into a funnel with a tip opening ½ inch in diameter. Keep the spout closed and control the flow of batter with the forefinger of your other hand. Dribble the batter directly into the hot oil, moving the funnel in a circle to build a snaillike coil of 3 or 4 rings about 6 inches in diameter. Form 2 or 3 cakes and deep-fry them for about 2 minutes on each side, turning them once with a slotted spatula. When the cakes are brown, arrange them side by side on the paper-lined pans and keep them warm in the oven. Repeat the procedure 4 or 5 times, using ½ cup batter for each batch. If the batter becomes stiff, add up to ¼ cup more milk a tablespoon at a time.

Serve the cakes warm, accompanied by molasses or maple syrup.

Apple Muffins

To make about 16 muffins

6 tablespoons butter, softened
2 cups unsifted flour
4 teaspoons double-acting baking powder
¼ teaspoon baking soda
½ teaspoon ground mace
½ teaspoon salt
¼ cup sugar

2 eggs
1 cup sour cream
3 medium-sized firm ripe cooking apples, 2 apples peeled, cored and finely chopped (about 1 cup) and 1 apple cored and cut lengthwise into ⅛-inch-thick slices

Preheat the oven to 425°. With a pastry brush, spread 2 tablespoons of softened butter evenly inside 16 muffin cups (each cup should be about 2½ inches across at the top). Combine the flour, baking powder, baking soda, mace and salt, and sift them together into a bowl. Set aside.

In a deep bowl, cream the remaining 4 tablespoons of butter and the sugar, beating and mashing them against the sides of the bowl with the back of a large spoon until the mixture is light and fluffy. Beat in the eggs, one at a time. Then add about 1 cup of the flour mixture and, when it is well incorporated, beat in ½ cup of the sour cream. Repeat, beating in the remaining flour and then the rest of the cream and stir until the batter is smooth. Stir in the chopped apples and spoon the batter into the muffin cups, filling each cup about halfway to the top. Insert a slice of apple, peel side up, partway into the top of each muffin.

Bake in the middle of the oven for 15 to 20 minutes, or until the muffins are brown and a cake tester or toothpick inserted in the centers comes out clean. Turn the muffins out of the tins and serve at once.

Blueberry Muffins

To make about twenty 2½-inch
  muffins

10 tablespoons butter, softened
2½ cups firm ripe blueberries
2 cups unsifted flour
2 teaspoons double-acting baking
  powder
½ teaspoon salt
1 cup sugar
2 eggs
½ cup milk

Preheat the oven to 375°. With a pastry brush, spread 2 tablespoons of the softened butter evenly inside 20 muffin cups (each cup should be about 2½ inches across at the top).

Wash the blueberries in a sieve or colander set under cold running water, discarding the stems and any blemished berries. Spread the berries on paper towels and pat them completely dry with more paper towels. Place ½ cup of the berries in a small bowl and mash them to a smooth purée with the back of a fork. Drop the rest of the berries into another bowl, add 2 tablespoons of the flour and toss gently about with a spoon to coat the berries evenly. Set aside.

Combine the remaining flour, the baking powder and salt, and sift them together onto a sheet of wax paper.

In a deep bowl, cream the remaining 8 tablespoons of butter with the sugar, beating and mashing them against the sides of the bowl with the back of a large spoon until the mixture is light and fluffy. Beat in the eggs, one at a time.

Add about 1 cup of the flour mixture and, when it is well incorporated, beat in ¼ cup of the milk. Repeat, beating in the remaining flour mixture and then the rest of the milk, and continue to mix until the batter is smooth. Add the puréed berries, beat well, then add the reserved whole berries and gently fold them into the batter with a rubber spatula.

Spoon the batter into the buttered muffin cups, filling each cup about ¾ full. Bake in the middle of the oven for 20 to 25 minutes, or until a cake tester or toothpick inserted in the center of a muffin comes out clean. Turn the muffins out of the tins and serve at once.

Philadelphia Cinnamon Buns

To make 14 buns

¼ cup lukewarm water (110° to
115°)
1 package active dry yeast
1 teaspoon plus ½ cup sugar
3 to 3½ cups unsifted flour
½ teaspoon salt
2 egg yolks

1 cup lukewarm milk (110° to
115°)
1 tablespoon butter, softened, plus
6 tablespoons butter, melted
1½ cups light brown sugar
½ cup light corn syrup
½ cup seedless raisins
2 teaspoons ground cinnamon

Pour the lukewarm water into a shallow bowl and sprinkle the yeast and
1 teaspoon of sugar over it. Let the mixture stand for 2 or 3 minutes,
then stir well. Set the bowl in a warm, draft-free place (such as an unlighted oven) for about 5 minutes, or until the yeast bubbles up and the
mixture almost doubles in volume.

Combine 3 cups of the flour, the remaining ½ cup of sugar and the
salt in a deep mixing bowl, and make a well in the center. Add the yeast
mixture, egg yolks and lukewarm milk. With a large spoon, slowly mix
the ingredients together, then stir until the dough is smooth and can be
gathered into a soft ball.

Place the ball on a lightly floured surface and knead, pushing the
dough down with the heels of your hands, pressing it forward and folding it back on itself. As you knead, sprinkle flour over the ball by the tablespoonful, adding up to ½ cup more flour if necessary to make a firm
dough. Continue to knead for about 10 minutes, or until the dough is
smooth, shiny and elastic.

With a pastry brush, spread the tablespoon of softened butter evenly inside a deep mixing bowl. Place the ball in the bowl and turn it around to
butter the entire surface of the dough. Drape the bowl loosely with a kitch-
en towel and put it in the draft-free place for about 1 hour, or until the
dough doubles in bulk.

In a small bowl, mix ¾ cup of light brown sugar, 2 tablespoons of
the melted butter, and the corn syrup to a smooth paste. Pour the mixture
into two 9-inch cake pans, tipping the pans back and forth to spread it
evenly. In another bowl, stir the remaining ¾ cup of light brown sugar,
the raisins and cinnamon together until they are well blended. Set aside.

Punch the dough down with a blow of your fist and, on a lightly
floured surface, roll it out into an 18-by-10-inch rectangle about ¼ inch
thick. Brush the surface of the dough with 2 tablespoons of the melted
butter and sprinkle it evenly with the sugar-and-raisin mixture.

Starting at one long side, roll the dough tightly into a cylinder about
18 inches long and 2½ inches in diameter. Then, with a sharp knife,
cut the cylinder crosswise into 14 rounds about 1¼ inch thick and 2½

inches in diameter. Place one round, cut side up, in the center of each sugar-lined cake pan and arrange the remaining rounds in circles of six around each center round. Set the buns aside in the draft-free place for about 45 minutes, or until they double in volume.

Preheat the oven to 350°. (If you have used the oven to let the buns rise, gently transfer them to a warm place to rest while the oven heats.) Brush the tops of the buns with the remaining 2 tablespoons of melted butter and bake in the middle of the oven for about 25 minutes, or until they are golden brown.

Place a wire cake rack over each pan and, grasping rack and pan together firmly, quickly invert them. Let the cinnamon buns cool to lukewarm before serving them.

Cottage-Cheese Pancakes

To make about 3 dozen 2-inch
    pancakes

1 cup creamed cottage cheese (8 ounces)	16 tablespoons butter (½ pound), melted and cooled
5 eggs, lightly beaten	1 teaspoon vanilla extract
½ cup unsifted flour	A pinch of salt

Preheat the oven to its lowest setting. Meanwhile, line a large baking sheet with paper towels and place it in the middle of the oven.

With the back of a spoon, rub the cottage cheese through a fine sieve into a deep mixing bowl. Beating constantly, pour in the eggs gradually and, when they are well incorporated, add the flour by the tablespoonful. Stir in 8 tablespoons of the cooled melted butter, the vanilla and salt.

Warm a large heavy griddle over moderate heat until a drop of water flicked onto it splutters and evaporates instantly. Grease the griddle lightly with a pastry brush dipped into the remaining 8 tablespoons of butter. Cook 5 or 6 pancakes at a time. To form each cake, pour about a tablespoon of the batter on the griddle, leaving enough space between them so that they can spread into 2-inch rounds. Fry them for 2 minutes on each side, or until they are golden and crisp around the edges.

As they brown, transfer the cakes to the paper-lined baking sheet and keep them warm in the oven while you fry the rest. Repeat the procedure, brushing the griddle with melted butter when necessary, until all the cottage-cheese pancakes are fried. Serve at once with jelly or jam.

Schwenkfelder Cake

To make two 9-inch round cakes

CAKE

2 cups water
1 medium-sized boiling potato,
    peeled and quartered
¼ teaspoon saffron threads,
    pulverized with a mortar and
    pestle or with the back of a spoon
    in a small bowl, or ¼ teaspoon
    ground saffron
1 package active dry yeast

¼ teaspoon plus ½ cup sugar
5 cups unsifted flour
½ teaspoon salt
½ cup lukewarm milk (110° to
    115°)
2 eggs
4 tablespoons butter, cut into ¼-
    inch bits and softened, plus 3
    tablespoons butter, softened

Bring the water to a boil over high heat in a small heavy saucepan. Add the potato and boil briskly, uncovered, until it can easily be pierced with a skewer or fork. Drain the potato quarters in a sieve set over a bowl, pat them dry with paper towels, and return the pieces to the pan. Mash the potato to a smooth purée with the back of a fork and cover the pan to keep the purée warm.

Pour ¾ cup of the hot potato water into a measuring cup, stir in the saffron and set aside to steep for 10 or 15 minutes. Pour ¼ cup of the remaining potato water into a shallow bowl and, when it has cooled to lukewarm, add the yeast and ¼ teaspoon of the sugar. (Discard the rest of the potato water.) Let the yeast mixture stand for 2 or 3 minutes, then stir well. Set the bowl in a warm, draft-free place (such as an unlighted oven) for about 5 minutes, or until the yeast bubbles up and the mixture almost doubles in volume.

Combine 4 cups of the flour, the remaining ½ cup of sugar and the salt in a deep mixing bowl, and make a well in the center. Add the potato purée, the yeast, the saffron water, the milk, eggs and 4 tablespoons of butter bits. With a large wooden spoon, gradually incorporate the dry ingredients into the liquid ones and beat until the dough is smooth and can be gathered into a compact ball.

Place the ball on a lightly floured surface and knead, pushing the dough down with the heels of your hands, pressing it forward and folding it back on itself. As you knead, sprinkle flour over the ball by the tablespoonful, adding up to 1 cup more flour if necessary to make a firm dough. Continue to knead for about 10 minutes, or until the dough is smooth, shiny and elastic.

With a pastry brush, spread 1 tablespoon of the softened butter evenly over the inside of a large bowl. Set the ball of dough in the bowl and turn it about to butter its entire surface. Drape the bowl loosely with a kitchen towel and put it in the draft-free place for 1½ hours, or until the dough doubles in volume.

Brush the bottoms and sides of two 9-inch layer-cake pans with the remaining 2 tablespoons of softened butter. Punch the dough down with a blow of your fist and divide it in half. On a lightly floured surface, pat and shape each half into a flat round about 8 inches in diameter and place the rounds in the buttered pans. Set the pans aside in the draft-free place for 30 to 45 minutes, or until the dough doubles in bulk.

Preheat the oven to 350°. (If you have used the oven to let the dough rise, transfer the pans gently to another warm place while the oven heats.)

CRUMB TOPPING
1¼ cups unsifted flour
1 cup light brown sugar
½ teaspoon ground cinnamon
8 tablespoons butter, cut into
    ¼-inch bits and chilled, plus
    2 tablespoons butter, melted

To prepare the crumb topping, combine 1¼ cups of flour, the brown sugar, cinnamon and 8 tablespoons of butter bits in a bowl. With your fingertips, rub the flour, sugar and butter together until they resemble flakes of coarse meal.

Brush the tops of the cakes with the 2 tablespoons of melted butter and sprinkle them evenly with the crumb mixture. Bake in the middle of the oven for 30 to 35 minutes, or until the tops are brown and crusty. Slide the Schwenkfelder cakes from the pans onto wire racks and let them cool before serving them.

Moravian Sugar Cake

To make two 16-by-11-inch cakes

2 cups water
2 medium-sized boiling potatoes, peeled and quartered
16 tablespoons butter, cut into ½-inch bits, plus 3 tablespoons butter, softened
1 package active dry yeast

1 teaspoon plus 1 cup granulated sugar
6 to 6½ cups unsifted flour
1 teaspoon salt
2 eggs
2¼ cups light brown sugar (1 pound)
2 teaspoons ground cinnamon

Bring the water to a boil in a small heavy saucepan, drop in the potatoes and boil briskly, uncovered, until they can be easily mashed against the side of the pan with the back of a fork. Drain the potatoes in a sieve set over a bowl, pat them dry with paper towels and return them to the pan. (Measure and reserve 1 cup of the potato water.) Then mash the potatoes to a smooth purée with the back of a fork. (You should have 1 cup of purée.) Beat in 8 tablespoons of the butter bits and cover the pan to keep the purée warm.

When the reserved potato water has cooled to lukewarm (110° to 115°), pour ¼ cup of it into a shallow bowl. Add the yeast and 1 teaspoon of the granulated sugar. Let the mixture stand for 2 or 3 minutes, then stir well. Set the bowl in a warm, draft-free place (such as an unlighted oven) for about 5 minutes, or until the yeast bubbles up and the mixture almost doubles in volume.

Combine 6 cups of the flour, the remaining cup of granulated sugar and the salt in a deep mixing bowl, and make a well in the center. Drop in the potato purée, the yeast mixture, the eggs and the remaining ¾ cup of potato water. With a large spoon, mix the ingredients together and stir until the dough is smooth and can be gathered into a soft ball. Place the ball on a lightly floured surface and knead, pushing the dough down with the heels of your hands, pressing it forward and folding it back on itself. As you knead, sprinkle flour over the ball a tablespoon at a time, adding up to ½ cup more flour if necessary to make a firm dough. Continue to knead for about 10 minutes, or until the dough is smooth, shiny and elastic, and gather it into a ball.

With a pastry brush, spread 1 tablespoon of softened butter evenly inside a deep mixing bowl. Place the ball in the bowl and turn it around to butter the entire surface of the dough. Drape the bowl loosely with a kitchen towel and put it in the draft-free place for about 1½ hours, or until the dough doubles in bulk.

Brush the remaining 2 tablespoons of softened butter over two 16-by-

11-inch jelly-roll pans. Punch the dough down with a single blow of your fist and divide it in half.

On a lightly floured surface, roll each half into a 16-by-11-inch rectangle about ½ inch thick. Place the dough in the buttered pans and set it aside in the draft-free place to rise again for about 45 minutes, or until it has doubled in bulk.

Preheat the oven to 350°. Stir the brown sugar and cinnamon together in a bowl. With your forefinger, make parallel rows of small indentations in the top of each cake, spacing the indentations about 1½ inches apart and pressing down almost to the bottom of the pan. Drop the remaining 8 tablespoons of butter bits into the indentations and fill the holes with brown-sugar mixture. Scatter the rest of the brown sugar over the surface of the cakes, dividing it evenly between them.

Bake in the middle of the oven for 25 to 30 minutes, or until the topping is golden brown and crusty. Transfer the Moravian sugar cakes to a platter and serve them warm or at room temperature.

Fastnachts

To make about 2 dozen doughnuts

2 cups water	1 package active dry yeast
1 medium-sized boiling potato, peeled and quartered	1 teaspoon plus 2½ cups sugar
	6 to 6½ cups unsifted flour
4 tablespoons butter, cut into ½-inch bits and softened, plus 2 teaspoons butter, softened	1 teaspoon salt
	2 eggs
	Vegetable oil for deep frying

In a small heavy saucepan, bring the water to a boil over high heat. Drop in the potato quarters and boil briskly, uncovered, until a quarter can be easily mashed against the side of the pan with the back of a fork.

Drain the potatoes in a sieve set over a bowl, pat them dry with a kitchen towel and return them to the pan. (Measure and reserve 1½ cups of the potato water.) Then mash the potatoes to a smooth purée with the back of a fork (you will need about ½ cup of the potato purée). Beat the 4 tablespoons of butter bits into the potatoes, and cover the pan to keep the purée warm.

When the reserved potato water has cooled to lukewarm (110° to 115°), pour ¼ cup of it into a shallow bowl. Add the yeast and 1 tea-

Continued on next page   101

spoon of sugar. Let the mixture stand for 2 or 3 minutes, then stir well. Set the bowl in a warm, draft-free place, such as an unlighted oven, for about 5 minutes, or until the yeast bubbles up and the mixture almost doubles in volume.

Combine 6 cups of the flour, ½ cup of the sugar and the salt in a deep mixing bowl, and make a well in the center. Drop in the potato purée, the yeast mixture, the eggs and the remaining 1¼ cups of potato water. With a large wooden spoon, mix the ingredients together and stir until the dough is smooth and can be gathered into a soft ball.

Place the ball on a lightly floured surface and knead, pushing the dough down with the heels of your hands, pressing it forward and folding it back on itself.

As you knead, sprinkle flour over the ball by the tablespoonful, adding up to ½ cup more flour if necessary to make a firm dough. Then continue to knead for about 10 minutes longer, or until the dough is smooth, shiny and elastic.

With a pastry brush, spread the 2 teaspoons of softened butter evenly over the inside of a large bowl. Set the dough in the bowl and turn it about to butter the entire surface. Drape the bowl with a kitchen towel and put it in the draft-free place for about 1½ hours, or until the dough doubles in bulk.

Line one or two large baking sheets with wax paper. Place the dough on a lightly floured surface and roll it out into a rough rectangle about ½ inch thick. With a small sharp knife or a pastry wheel, cut the dough into 2-inch squares, and make a 1-inch slash in the center of each. Arrange the squares about 1 inch apart on the paper-lined baking sheet and return them to the draft-free place to rise for 30 to 45 minutes, or until doubled in bulk.

Pour vegetable oil into a deep fryer or large heavy saucepan to a depth of 3 inches and heat it to a temperature of 375° on a deep-frying thermometer. At the same time, place about ½ cup of the remaining sugar in a paper bag and set it aside.

Deep-fry the dough squares 4 or 5 at a time, turning them with a slotted spoon, for 3 minutes, or until they are puffed and brown. Drain the *fastnachts,* or doughnuts, briefly on paper towels, then drop two at a time into the bag and shake to coat them with sugar. (Add more sugar to the bag as needed.) Place the *fastnachts* on a platter to cool while you fry and sugar the rest.

PICKLES, PRESERVES & RELISHES

Bread-and-Butter Pickles

To make 3 to 4 quarts

5 pounds firm ripe cucumbers (about 10 medium-sized cucumbers), scrubbed, trimmed of ends and cut crosswise into ¼-inch-thick rounds
3 medium-sized onions, peeled and cut crosswise into ¼-inch-thick slices
1 large green bell pepper, washed, halved, seeded, deribbed and cut into 2-by-¼-inch strips
1 large red bell pepper, washed, halved, seeded, deribbed and cut into 2-by-¼-inch strips
1 cup salt
6 cups sugar
3 cups distilled white vinegar
1 tablespoon celery seeds
1 tablespoon celery salt

Combine the cucumbers, onions, and green and red peppers in a large colander set over a bowl. Sprinkle with the salt, turning the vegetables about with a wooden spoon to coat them evenly. Let the vegetable mixture stand at room temperature for 2 to 3 hours to allow the excess liquid to drain. Then place the colander under cold running water and wash off the salt, tossing the vegetables about with the spoon. Set the colander aside and let the vegetables drain.

In a 6- to 8-quart enameled casserole, bring the sugar, vinegar, celery seeds and celery salt to a boil over high heat, stirring with a wooden spoon until the sugar dissolves. Add the vegetables handful by handful, and return the liquid to the boil. Boil the vegetables briskly, uncovered and undisturbed, for about 2 minutes.

Remove the pan from the heat and ladle the pickle mixture immediately into hot sterilized jars, filling them to within ¼ inch of the top. Following the directions for home canning on page 3, seal and process the jars for 15 minutes in a boiling-water bath.

Chowchow

To make 7 to 8 quarts

6 quarts water
1 cup dried navy beans
1 cup dried red kidney beans
2 pounds shelled fresh Lima beans
1 pound fresh green string beans, trimmed, washed and cut into 1-inch pieces
1½ pounds fresh yellow wax beans, trimmed, washed and cut into 1-inch pieces
A 1- to 1¼-pound head fresh cauliflower, trimmed, washed and broken into small flowerets
A 1- to 1¼-pound bunch celery, trimmed, leaves removed, washed and cut into 1-inch pieces

1 pound green bell peppers, halved, seeded, deribbed and cut into 2-by-¼-inch strips
1 pound red bell peppers, halved, seeded, deribbed and cut into 2-by-¼-inch strips
6 cups fresh corn kernels, cut from 10 to 12 large ears of corn
16 cups sugar
2 quarts distilled white vinegar
¼ cup mustard seeds
2 teaspoons celery seeds
1 teaspoon turmeric
2 two-inch pieces stick cinnamon and 1 tablespoon whole cloves, wrapped together in cheesecloth

Traditionally, Pennsylvania Dutch housewives cook the vegetables for chowchow separately. Though this may seem tedious, the technique ensures that each vegetable keeps its shape and color and is properly crunchy. You may want to combine vegetables to speed the process, but, if you do, keep a close eye on the pot to prevent overcooking them.

In a heavy 3- to 4-quart saucepan, bring 2 quarts of the water to a boil over high heat. Drop in the dried navy and kidney beans, and boil them briskly, uncovered, for about 2 minutes. (The water should cover the beans by at least 2 inches; if necessary, add more water.)

Turn off the heat and let the beans soak for 1 hour. Then bring to a boil again and reduce the heat to low. Simmer partially covered for about 1 hour, or until the beans are tender. Check the pan from time to time and add more boiling water if needed. Drain the beans through a fine sieve, discarding the cooking liquid, and set them aside.

Meanwhile, bring 4 quarts of water to a boil in an 8- to 10-quart enameled pot. Drop in the Lima beans. When the water returns to a boil, cook the beans briskly for 20 to 30 minutes, or until they are tender but still crisp to the bite. With a slotted spoon, scoop the beans out of the water into a colander or sieve and run cold water over them for a minute or so to set their color and stop their cooking. Drain well and set the Limas aside in a 10- to 12-quart pot.

Return the water in the pot to a boil over high heat. Then drop in the string beans and wax beans, a handful at a time so that the boiling never stops. Cook briskly, uncovered, for 8 to 10 minutes, or until the beans are barely tender. With a slotted spoon, transfer them to a colander or sieve and run cold water over them briefly. Let them drain for a minute or so, then add them to the Lima beans. Return the cooking water to a boil again and in similar fashion boil the cauliflower, the celery, the green and red peppers, and the corn separately, running cold water over each vegetable and adding it to the Lima beans as soon as it is cooked. Allow about 8 to 10 minutes for the cauliflower, 5 to 6 minutes for the celery, 5 minutes for the green and red peppers, and 4 to 5 minutes for the corn.

Add the cooked navy and kidney beans to the vegetable mixture and, with a wooden spoon, toss gently but thoroughly together. Pack the vegetables into sterilized jars, dividing them evenly, according to the directions for home canning on page 3.

Combine the sugar, vinegar, mustard seeds, celery seeds, turmeric, and the wrapped cinnamon and cloves in a 5- to 6-quart enameled saucepan and bring to a boil over high heat, stirring until the sugar dissolves. Cook briskly for 5 minutes.

Remove the pan from the heat and discard the bag of cinnamon and cloves. Ladle the hot syrup over the vegetables, a few tablespoonfuls at a time, allowing the liquid and spices to flow through to the bottom of the jars before adding more, and filling the jars to within ¼ inch of the top. Following the directions for home canning on page 3, process the jars 15 minutes in a boiling-water bath.

Ground-Cherry Jam

To make 1 pint

2 cups husked, fully ripe ground
   cherries, washed
1 tablespoon finely grated fresh
lemon peel
¼ cup water
2 cups sugar
3 tablespoons liquid fruit pectin

Ground cherries are not cherries at all, but the edible berries of low, sprawling, bushy plants that often appear wild although they may be grown from seed. Enclosed in a papery Japanese lanternlike husk, the berry is also known as a husk tomato, strawberry tomato or dwarf cape gooseberry. It is smooth, greenish yellow or orange when ripe, and about ½ inch in diameter.

Drop the ground cherries into a heavy 3- to 4-quart enameled saucepan and crush them lightly with the back of a wooden spoon. Add the lemon peel and water and bring to a boil over high heat. Then cook briskly, uncovered, for 5 minutes, or until a ground cherry can be easily mashed against the side of the pot with the back of the spoon.

Stirring constantly, add the sugar and boil vigorously for 1 minute. Remove the pan from the heat and immediately stir in the liquid pectin. Carefully skim off the surface foam with a large spoon. Ladle the jam into hot sterilized jars or jelly glasses and seal them at once, following the directions for home canning on page 3.

Crab-Apple Jelly

To make 3 or 4 cups

8 cups fresh crab apples (about
   2 pounds)
6 cups water
2 to 3 cups sugar

Pick over the crab apples carefully, removing the stems and discarding any badly blemished fruit. Wash the crab apples in a colander under cold running water and drop them into a 6- to 8-quart enameled pot. Add 6 cups of water and bring to a boil over high heat. Reduce the heat to low, cover the pot tightly, and simmer for 30 minutes, or until a crab apple can be mashed easily against the side of the pot with the back of a spoon.

Line a colander or sieve with four layers of damp cheesecloth and place it over a large enameled pot. The bottom of the colander or sieve should be suspended above the pot by at least 3 inches. Pour in the crab apples and, without disturbing them, allow the juice to drain through into the pot. (Do not squeeze the cloth or the jelly will be cloudy.)

When the juice has drained through completely, measure and return it to the first enameled pot. Discard the crab apples. Depending on the tartness of the juice, add from ¾ to 1 cup of sugar for each cup of juice. Bring to a boil over high heat, stirring until the sugar dissolves. Cook briskly, uncovered and undisturbed, until the jelly reaches a temperature of 220° (or 8° above the boiling point of water in your locality) on a jelly, candy or deep-frying thermometer.

Remove the pot from the heat and carefully skim off the surface foam with a large spoon. Ladle the jelly into hot sterilized jars or jelly glasses, following the directions for home canning on page 3.

Apple Butter

To make about 3 pints

5 pounds tart cooking apples, peeled, quartered and cored	3 cups apple cider 4 cups sugar

Combine the apples and cider in a 4- to 5-quart enameled or stainless-steel pot and bring to a boil over high heat. Reduce the heat to low. Simmer partially covered for 20 to 25 minutes, or until an apple quarter can be easily mashed against the side of the pot with a fork.

Preheat the oven to 300°. Purée the apples through the finest blade of a food mill set over a deep bowl, or rub them through a fine sieve with the back of a spoon. Add the sugar and mix well.

Pour the apple purée into a shallow 14-by-8-inch baking dish, spreading it evenly and smoothing the top with a rubber spatula. Bake in the middle of the oven for about 2 hours, or until the apple butter is thick enough to hold its shape solidly in a spoon.

The traditional test for doneness is to dab a spoonful of the apple butter on a plate and turn the plate upside down. The apple butter should be thick enough to adhere to the inverted plate.

At once ladle the apple butter into hot sterilized jars, filling them to within ⅛ inch of the top. Seal the jars immediately, following the directions for home canning on page 3.

Pennsylvania Pepper Relish

To make about 4 cups

2 cups finely chopped white cabbage
1 cup finely chopped green bell
 peppers
1 cup finely chopped red bell
 peppers
1 cup finely chopped celery
3 tablespoons salt
1 cup distilled white vinegar
½ cup water
3 tablespoons dark brown sugar
2 tablespoons mustard seeds

Combine the cabbage, green and red peppers, celery and salt in a deep heatproof bowl and mix well with a wooden spoon. Transfer the vegetables to a colander and stand the colander in the bowl. Cover the colander with foil or plastic wrap, set aside at room temperature for 12 hours to allow the excess moisture to drain off. Discard the liquid and return the vegetables to the bowl.

In a small enameled or stainless-steel saucepan, bring the vinegar, water, brown sugar and mustard seeds to a boil over high heat, stirring until the sugar dissolves completely. Pour the hot vinegar mixture over the vegetables and turn them about with a spoon until they are evenly moistened. Cool to room temperature and serve the pepper relish at once. Or cool, cover with foil, and refrigerate the relish until ready to serve.

Spiced Cantaloupe

To make 1 quart

A 2-pound firm ripe cantaloupe
⅔ cup sugar
⅓ cup water
3 tablespoons distilled white
 vinegar
A 2-inch stick cinnamon
4 whole cloves

Cut the cantaloupe into quarters and, with a spoon, scoop out the seeds and stringy pulp. With a small sharp knife, remove the skin and the inner rind. Then cut the meat into 2-inch pieces, and pack the pieces into a 1-quart canning jar.

Combine the sugar, water, vinegar, cinnamon and cloves in a 2-quart enameled or stainless-steel saucepan and bring to a boil over high heat, stirring until the sugar dissolves. Cook briskly, uncovered, for 5 minutes.

With tongs, remove the cinnamon stick and tuck it down the side of the cantaloupe-filled jar. Then ladle the hot liquid over the cantaloupe, a few tablespoonfuls at a time, allowing the liquid to flow through to the bottom of the jar before adding more. Fill the jar to within ⅛ inch of the top. Following the directions for home canning on page 3, seal and process the jar for 12 minutes in a boiling-water bath.

Red Beet Eggs

To serve 6

3 cups water	1 cup sugar
1 pound small firm fresh beets, each about 1½ to 2 inches in diameter, peeled and trimmed	½ cup distilled white vinegar 6 hard-cooked eggs, peeled and cooled

In a 2- to 3-quart enameled saucepan, bring the water to a boil over high heat. Drop in the beets, reduce the heat to low and cover the pan tightly. Simmer for 30 to 40 minutes, or until the beets show no resistance when pierced with the point of a small sharp knife.

With a slotted spoon, transfer the beets to a plate. Add the sugar and vinegar to the beet juice and bring to a boil, stirring until the sugar dissolves. Return the beets to the pan and, turning them frequently, cook over low heat for about 5 minutes.

Drain the beets in a sieve set over a deep bowl and put them aside. Add the eggs to the beet juice and turn them about with a spoon to moisten them evenly. Place the beets on top of the eggs. Cool to room temperature, then cover tightly with foil or plastic wrap and marinate in the refrigerator for about 12 hours before serving.

To serve, remove the eggs from the beet juice and pat them dry with paper towels. Cut the eggs lengthwise into halves and arrange them attractively on a platter. Slice the beets ¼ inch thick and put them into a serving bowl. Pour in the juice and serve the beets from the bowl.

Pepper Cabbage

To serve 6

A 1-pound green cabbage
½ cup cold water
5 tablespoons distilled white
  vinegar
¼ cup sugar

1 teaspoon salt
½ cup finely chopped green bell
  pepper
½ cup finely chopped celery
¼ cup grated scraped carrot

Wash the head of cabbage under cold running water, remove the tough outer leaves, and cut the cabbage into quarters. To shred the cabbage, cut out the core and slice the quarters crosswise into ⅛-inch-wide strips.

Combine the water, vinegar, sugar and salt in a deep bowl and stir until the sugar dissolves.

Add the cabbage, green pepper, celery and carrot, and toss together gently but thoroughly. Then cover the bowl tightly with plastic wrap and marinate the vegetables in the refrigerator for 3 to 4 hours. Just before serving, toss the pepper cabbage again and taste for seasoning.

Pennsylvania Dutch Coleslaw

To serve 4 to 6

1 cup sugar
½ cup cider vinegar
2 teaspoons celery salt

¼ teaspoon salt
½ cup finely chopped red bell
  pepper
A 1½- to 2-pound green cabbage

Combine the sugar, vinegar, celery salt and salt in a small bowl and stir until the sugar and salt dissolve. Add the red pepper and mix well.

Wash the cabbage under cold water, remove the tough outer leaves, and cut the cabbage lengthwise into quarters. Shred the cabbage by cutting out the core and slicing the quarters crosswise into ⅛-inch strips.

Drop the shredded cabbage into a serving bowl, pour the sugar and vinegar dressing over the cabbage, and toss together gently but thoroughly. Taste for seasoning and serve at once.

NUTS

Spiced Mixed Nuts

To make about 1 pound

1 tablespoon butter, softened
¾ cup sugar
1 teaspoon ground cinnamon
½ teaspoon ground cloves
¼ teaspoon ground nutmeg
¼ teaspoon ground ginger
¼ teaspoon ground allspice

½ teaspoon salt
1 egg white, lightly beaten
2 tablespoons cold water
1 cup whole blanched unsalted
  almonds
1 cup unsalted broken black walnuts
½ cup whole unsalted filberts

Preheat the oven to 275°. With a pastry brush, spread the tablespoon of softened butter over a large baking sheet. Combine the sugar, cinnamon, cloves, nutmeg, ginger, allspice and salt in a small bowl and mix well. Add the egg white and water and stir until the mixture is a smooth paste. With a table fork, stir in about ½ cup of the nuts and, when they are evenly coated, transfer one at a time to the baking sheet. Coat the remaining nuts by the half cupful and arrange on the sheet in one layer.

Bake the nuts in the middle of the oven for 45 minutes, or until the spice coating is crisp and golden brown. Cool to room temperature and store the spiced mixed nuts in a tightly covered jar until ready to serve.

Sherried Walnuts

To make about ½ pound

1 tablespoon butter, softened	½ teaspoon ground cinnamon
1½ cups sugar	⅛ teaspoon ground nutmeg
½ cup dry sherry	2 cups unsalted walnut halves

With a pastry brush, spread the tablespoon of softened butter over a large baking sheet and set it aside.

Combine the sugar and sherry in a heavy 1-quart enameled saucepan and bring to a boil over high heat, stirring until the sugar dissolves. Then cook briskly, uncovered and undisturbed, until the syrup reaches a temperature of 240° on a candy thermometer or until about ⅛ teaspoon of the syrup dropped into ice water instantly forms a soft ball.

At once remove the pan from the heat and add the cinnamon, nutmeg and walnut halves. Stir gently for a few minutes, until the syrup becomes opaque and creamy. While the mixture is still soft, spread it on the buttered baking sheet and, with two table forks, carefully separate the candy-coated walnut halves. Set the sherried walnuts aside to cool to room temperature, then store in a tightly covered jar until ready to serve.

Toasted Pecans

To make about 1 pound

6 tablespoons butter, cut into ½-inch bits	1 pound (about 4 cups) whole unsalted pecans
	1 tablespoon salt

Preheat the oven to 350°. In a heavy 8- to 10-inch skillet, melt the butter over moderate heat. When the foam subsides remove the pan from the heat, add the pecans and stir until they glisten with butter.

Spread the pecans in one layer in a jelly-roll pan or shallow baking dish. Toast the nuts in the middle of the oven for 15 to 20 minutes, stirring and turning them occasionally. When the nuts are crisp and brown, remove the pan from the oven, add the salt and toss the nuts about gently to season them evenly.

Cool to room temperature and store the toasted pecans in a tightly covered jar until ready to serve.

Mixed-Nut Brittle

To make about 2 pounds

1 cup whole unsalted blanched
   almonds
1 cup unsalted broken black walnuts
½ cup whole unsalted filberts
1 teaspoon salt
1 tablespoon butter, softened, plus
   2 tablespoons butter, cut into bits
1½ cups sugar
1 cup light corn syrup
⅓ cup water
1 teaspoon vanilla extract

Preheat the oven to 350°. Mix the almonds, black walnuts, filberts and salt in a large shallow baking dish. Toast the nuts in the middle of the oven for about 5 minutes, stirring them from time to time. Then turn off the heat, but leave the nuts in the oven to keep them warm.

With a pastry brush, spread the tablespoon of softened butter over a large baking sheet and set it aside. Combine the sugar, corn syrup and water in a heavy 2- to 3-quart saucepan and bring to a boil over high heat, stirring until the sugar dissolves. Then cook briskly, uncovered and undisturbed, until the syrup reaches a temperature of 290° on a candy thermometer or until about ⅛ teaspoon of the syrup dropped into ice water immediately separates into hard but not brittle threads.

Remove the pan from the heat and immediately beat in the 2 table-spoons of butter bits, the vanilla and the warm nuts. Pour the candy onto the buttered baking sheet and set it aside to cool to room temperature. Break the mixed-nut brittle into pieces with a kitchen mallet or your hands, and store in a tightly covered jar until ready to serve.

 # DESERTS

Apple Jonathan

To serve 6 to 8

5 tablespoons butter, softened
1 cup flour
2 teaspoons double-acting baking
powder
½ teaspoon salt
½ cup sugar
1 egg

¼ cup milk
6 medium-sized tart cooking apples
(about 2 pounds), peeled, cored
and cut lengthwise into ⅛-inch-
thick slices
½ cup pure maple syrup
1 cup heavy cream

Preheat the oven to 400°. With a pastry brush, spread 1 tablespoon of the softened butter evenly over the bottom and sides of a shallow 3-quart baking dish. Combine the flour, baking powder and salt, and sift them together onto a plate or a sheet of wax paper.

In a deep bowl, cream the remaining 4 tablespoons of butter and the sugar, beating and mashing the mixture against the sides of the bowl with the back of a spoon until it is light and fluffy. Beat in the egg. Add about ½ cup of the flour mixture and, when it is well incorporated, stir in 2 tablespoons of the milk. Then beat in the remaining ½ cup of flour and the remaining 2 tablespoons of milk and stir until the batter is smooth.

Drop the apple slices into a bowl, pour in the maple syrup, and stir until the slices are coated on all sides. Spread the apple slices evenly in the bottom of the buttered baking dish and pour in the batter, smoothing the top with a rubber spatula.

Bake in the middle of the oven for 30 to 35 minutes, or until a cake tester or toothpick inserted in the topping comes out clean. Serve the apple Jonathan hot or at room temperature, spooning it out of the baking dish into individual dessert bowls. Present the cream separately in a pitcher.

Peach Custard

To serve 6

3 medium-sized firm ripe peaches	¼ cup sugar
1 cup heavy cream	1 teaspoon vanilla extract
1 cup milk	¼ teaspoon ground nutmeg,
3 eggs plus 2 egg yolks	preferably freshly grated

Preheat the oven to 325°. Drop the peaches into enough boiling water to immerse them completely and boil briskly, uncovered, for 2 or 3 minutes. With a slotted spoon, transfer the peaches to a sieve or colander and run cold water over them. Peel the peaches with a small sharp knife, halve them and remove the pits. Place each peach half, cut side down, in a 6-ounce custard cup and set aside.

In a small heavy saucepan, warm the cream and milk over moderate heat until small bubbles appear around the sides of the pan. Remove the pan from the heat and cover to keep warm.

With a wire whisk or a rotary or electric beater, beat the eggs and additional egg yolks together in a bowl for 2 or 3 minutes. When they begin to thicken and cling to the beater, beat in the sugar. Then, beating the mixture constantly, pour in the warm cream-and-milk mixture in a slow, thin stream. Add the vanilla and pour the custard mixture over the peaches. Sprinkle the tops with the nutmeg.

Arrange the custard cups in a large shallow baking pan set in the middle of the oven. Pour enough boiling water into the pan to come about 1 inch up the sides of the cups. Bake for 30 to 40 minutes, or until a knife inserted in the custard comes out clean. Remove the cups from the baking pan, cool to room temperature, and serve at once. Or refrigerate and serve the peach custard chilled.

Raspberry Cream Roll

To make one 15-inch cake roll

2 tablespoons butter, softened
2 tablespoons plus ½ cup unsifted
   flour
⅛ teaspoon salt
4 egg whites

4 egg yolks
½ cup granulated sugar
½ teaspoon vanilla extract
2 cups ripe fresh raspberries
2 cups heavy cream, chilled
3 tablespoons confectioners' sugar

Preheat the oven to 400°. With a pastry brush, spread 1 tablespoon of the softened butter over the bottom and sides of a 16-by-11-inch jelly-roll pan. Line the pan with a 20-inch-long strip of wax paper and let the extra paper extend over the edges. Brush the remaining tablespoon of butter over the paper in the pan and sprinkle it with 2 tablespoons of the flour. Tip the pan from side to side to spread the flour evenly, then turn the pan over and rap it sharply to remove the excess flour. Combine the remaining ½ cup of flour with the salt and sift them together on a plate or piece of wax paper. Set aside.

With a wire whisk or a rotary or electric beater, beat the egg whites until they are stiff enough to stand in unwavering peaks on the beater when it is lifted from the bowl. In another bowl and with the same beater, beat the egg yolks, ¼ cup of the granulated sugar and the vanilla together for 4 or 5 minutes, until the mixture is thick.

Sprinkle the sifted flour on top of the egg whites, pour the yolk mixture over them and, with a rubber spatula, fold together lightly but thoroughly, using an over-under cutting motion rather than a stirring motion.

Pour the batter into the paper-lined pan, spread it into the corners with the spatula and smooth the top. Bake in the middle of the oven for 15 minutes, or until the cake begins to shrink from the sides of the pan and a cake tester or toothpick inserted in the center comes out clean.

Remove the pan from the oven and carefully turn the cake out onto a fresh sheet of wax paper. Gently peel off the layer of paper from the top of the cake and trim the edges of the cake with a sharp knife. Starting at one long edge, roll the cake into a loose cylinder. Set aside to cool to room temperature.

Wash the raspberries in a sieve or colander set under cold running water and pick out and discard any bruised or blemished berries. Spread the berries on paper towels to drain and pat them dry with paper towels.

In a chilled bowl, whip the cream with a wire whisk or a rotary or electric beater until the cream thickens lightly. Add the remaining ¼ cup of granulated sugar and continue to beat until the cream is stiff enough to form unwavering peaks on the beater when it is lifted from the bowl.

Ladle about ½ cup of the cream into a pastry bag fitted with a star tube. With a rubber spatula, fold 1½ cups of the raspberries into the remaining cream.

To assemble the cake, unroll it and spread the top evenly with the raspberry cream. Carefully roll up the cake again and place it on a serving plate. Sprinkle the roll evenly with the confectioners' sugar and pipe rosettes of cream on top. Decorate each rosette with one of the reserved raspberries. Serve at once or refrigerate until ready to serve.

Strawberry Flummery

To serve 4 to 6

	3 cups milk
½ cup plus 2 tablespoons sugar	1 egg yolk, lightly beaten
⅓ cup cornstarch	1 teaspoon vanilla extract
¼ teaspoon salt	1 pint firm ripe strawberries

Combine ½ cup of the sugar, the cornstarch and salt in a heavy 2- to 3-quart saucepan and, stirring the mixture constantly with a wire whisk, pour in the milk in a slow, thin stream. Whisking constantly, cook over moderate heat until the mixture comes to a boil and thickens heavily. Reduce the heat to its lowest setting.

Ladle several tablespoonfuls of the liquid into the beaten egg yolk, mix well and, still whisking, gradually pour the yolk into the simmering liquid. Simmer for 3 or 4 minutes longer to cook the egg yolk through, but do not let the mixture come anywhere near a boil.

Remove the pan from the heat and stir in the vanilla. Cool to room temperature, then pour the flummery into a serving bowl. Cover with wax paper and refrigerate for at least 2 hours, or until the flummery is thoroughly chilled.

Just before serving, pick over the strawberries, removing the hulls and discarding any blemished berries. Wash the strawberries briefly in a sieve or colander set under cold running water. Spread the berries on paper towels and pat them completely dry with fresh towels. Cut each berry in half lengthwise. Place the halves in a bowl, add the remaining 2 tablespoons of sugar, and toss gently together with a wooden spoon to coat the berries evenly. Arrange the strawberries attractively on top of the flummery and serve at once.

Floating Island

To serve 8 to 10

MERINGUE AND CUSTARD	2 to 2¼ cups light cream
5 egg whites	A 2-inch piece of vanilla bean
½ cup plus ⅔ cup sugar	5 egg yolks

With a wire whisk or a rotary or electric beater, beat the egg whites. As soon as they are frothy, add ½ cup of the sugar. Then continue to beat until the meringue is stiff enough to stand in unwavering peaks on the beater when it is lifted from the bowl.

In a heavy 8- to 10-inch skillet, heat 2 cups of cream and the vanilla bean over low heat. When small bubbles begin to form around the sides of the pan, reduce the heat to the lowest point.

To form each "island" scoop up the meringue in one dessert spoon and invert another dessert spoon over it to shape the meringue into an oval. Slide the meringue off the spoon onto the surface of the simmering cream. Make similar ovals of the remaining meringue. Simmer the meringues uncovered for 2 minutes, turn them over gently with a slotted spoon and cook for 1 or 2 minutes longer, or until they are just firm to the touch. Do not overcook the meringues, or they might disintegrate. Transfer the meringues to a kitchen towel to drain and let them cool to room temperature.

Strain the cream through a fine sieve, measure it and add enough more cream to make 2 cups. Return the vanilla bean and set the cream aside.

Combine the egg yolks and ⅔ cup of sugar in a heavy 2- to 3-quart saucepan and beat them together with a wire whisk. Whisking the mixture constantly, pour in the cream in a slow, thin stream. Add the vanilla bean and place the pan over low heat. Stir gently with a spoon until the custard coats the spoon heavily. Do not let the custard come anywhere near a boil or it will curdle. Strain the custard through a fine sieve into a bowl, discarding the vanilla bean. Cool to room temperature, then refrigerate the custard for 3 to 4 hours to chill it thoroughly.

| CARAMEL | |
| ⅔ cup sugar | ⅓ cup water |

About half an hour before serving, prepare the caramel. Combine ⅔ cup of sugar and ⅓ cup of water in a small heavy pan and bring to a boil over high heat, stirring until the sugar dissolves. Boil the syrup over moderate heat, gently tipping the pan back and forth until the syrup turns a tealike brown. This may take 10 minutes or more. Immediately remove the pan from the heat and pour the caramel into a bowl.

Arrange the meringues on top of the custard and, when the caramel is lukewarm, dribble it over them with a small spoon. To serve, ladle the meringues onto individual dessert plates and spoon custard around them.

Indiana Persimmon Pudding

To serve 4 to 6

1 tablespoon butter, softened, plus 2 tablespoons butter, melted and cooled
1 cup unsifted flour
1 teaspoon baking soda
½ teaspoon ground cinnamon
½ teaspoon ground ginger
¼ teaspoon ground nutmeg,

preferably freshly grated
1 pound (about 2 dozen) fully ripe wild persimmons
1 cup sugar
½ cup milk
1 teaspoon vanilla extract
½ cup seedless raisins
½ cup heavy cream, chilled and whipped

Preheat the oven to 350°. With a pastry brush, spread the tablespoon of softened butter evenly over the bottom and sides of a 1-quart soufflé dish.

Combine the flour, soda, cinnamon, ginger and nutmeg, and sift them together onto a plate or a sheet of wax paper. Set aside.

Wash the persimmons gently under cold running water and pat them dry with paper towels. With a small sharp knife, cut the persimmons into quarters and pick out the seeds. Purée the fruit through a food mill set over a deep bowl, or rub through a coarse sieve with the back of a spoon. You will need about 1 cup of puréed persimmons.

Add the sugar to the purée and mix well with a wooden spoon. Stir in about ½ cup of the flour mixture and, when it is thoroughly incorporated add ¼ cup of the milk. Stir in the remaining ½ cup of flour mixture and then the rest of the milk, beating well after each addition. Add the 2 tablespoons of melted, cooled butter, the vanilla and raisins.

Pour the batter into the buttered soufflé dish, spreading it evenly with a rubber spatula. Bake in the middle of the oven for 50 to 60 minutes, or until the pudding begins to shrink away from the sides of the dish and a cake tester or toothpick inserted in the center comes out clean.

Serve the persimmon pudding at once, directly from the baking dish. Spoon the whipped cream into a serving bowl and present it separately.

Lemon Rice Pudding

To serve 4 to 6

1 cup uncooked long-grain white
   rice, not the converted variety
¾ cup sugar
½ cup seedless raisins
½ teaspoon salt
4½ to 5 cups milk
2 egg yolks, lightly beaten
1 teaspoon finely grated fresh lemon
   peel
1 teaspoon vanilla extract

Combine the rice, sugar, raisins, salt and 4½ cups of milk in a heavy 3- to 4-quart saucepan. Bring the mixture to a boil over high heat, stirring until the sugar dissolves. Then reduce the heat to its lowest setting and cover the pan tightly. Simmer for 45 minutes, until the rice is soft and a grain can be easily mashed against the side of the pan with the back of a spoon. (Check the pan from time to time and, if the liquid seems to be cooking away, stir in up to ½ cup more milk by the tablespoonful.)

When the rice is fully cooked, ladle about 2 tablespoons of the hot liquid into the beaten egg yolks and mix well. Then, stirring the rice mixture constantly, pour in the egg yolks and cook gently over low heat for 2 to 3 minutes longer. Do not let the mixture come anywhere near a boil or it will curdle.

Remove the pan from the heat, stir in the lemon peel and vanilla, and pour the rice pudding into a serving bowl to cool to room temperature. Refrigerate the pudding for 1 or 2 hours, or until thoroughly chilled.

Cracker Pudding

To serve 6 to 8

1 quart milk
2 egg yolks
⅔ cup sugar
2 cups fine crumbs made from
    saltine crackers pulverized in a
    blender or placed between sheets
    of wax paper and crushed with a
    rolling pin
A 3½-ounce can flaked moist
    coconut (1¼ cups)
1 teaspoon vanilla extract
2 egg whites

In a heavy 3- to 4-quart saucepan, heat the milk until small bubbles begin to appear around the sides of the pan. Remove the pan from the heat and cover to keep the milk warm.

With a wire whisk or a rotary or electric beater, beat the egg yolks and sugar together for 3 or 4 minutes, until they are thick enough to fall in a ribbon from the beater when it is lifted out of the bowl. Beating constantly, pour the milk into the egg yolks in a slow thin stream. When thoroughly blended, return the mixture to the saucepan. Add the cracker crumbs and coconut, and stir over low heat until the custard thickens enough to coat a spoon or reaches 180° on a candy thermometer. Do not let it come anywhere near a boil or the custard will curdle. Remove the pan from the heat and stir in the vanilla.

Immediately beat the egg whites with a wire whisk or a rotary or electric beater until they are stiff enough to stand in unwavering peaks on the beater when it is lifted from the bowl. With a rubber spatula, scoop the egg whites over the warm custard and fold them together gently but thoroughly. Serve at once, or cool the cracker pudding to room temperature before serving.

Blueberry Crumb Cake

To serve 10 to 12

9 tablespoons butter, softened, plus 8 tablespoons butter, chilled and cut into ¼-inch bits
2 tablespoons plus 3¼ cups unsifted flour
2 cups sugar
1 teaspoon ground cinnamon
3 cups firm ripe blueberries

1 tablespoon double-acting baking powder
½ teaspoon ground nutmeg
¼ teaspoon ground cloves
1 teaspoon salt
3 eggs
¾ cup milk
2 cups heavy cream

Preheat the oven to 375°. With a pastry brush, spread 1 tablespoon of softened butter over the bottom and sides of a 13-by-9-by-3-inch baking dish. Add 2 tablespoons of the flour and tip the dish to spread it evenly. Invert the dish and rap the bottom sharply to remove excess flour.

Prepare the crumb topping by combining the 8 tablespoons of butter bits, ¾ cup of the flour, 1 cup of the sugar and the cinnamon in a deep bowl. Working quickly, rub the flour and fat together with your fingertips until the mixture resembles flakes of coarse meal. Set aside.

Wash the blueberries in a colander under cold running water. Remove the stems and discard any berries that are badly bruised. Spread the berries on paper towels and pat them completely dry with fresh towels.

Combine the remaining 2½ cups of flour, the baking powder, nutmeg, cloves and salt, and sift them together into a bowl.

In a deep bowl, cream the remaining 8 tablespoons of softened butter and 1 cup of sugar by beating and mashing them against the sides of the bowl with the back of a spoon until they are light and fluffy. Beat in the eggs, one at a time. Add about 1 cup of the sifted flour mixture and, when it is well incorporated, stir in ¼ cup of the milk. Repeat twice more, alternating 1 cup of the flour with ¼ cup of milk and beating well after each addition. Gently stir in the blueberries.

Pour the blueberry batter into the buttered-and-floured baking dish, spreading it evenly and smoothing the top with a rubber spatula. Then sprinkle the reserved crumb topping evenly over the cake.

Bake in the middle of the oven for 40 to 50 minutes, or until the top is crusty and a toothpick or cake tester inserted in the center of the cake comes out clean. Serve the blueberry crumb cake warm or at room temperature, and present the cream separately in a pitcher.

Chocolate Ice Cream

To make about 2 quarts

1 quart heavy cream
8 ounces semisweet baking
   chocolate, coarsely chopped
1 tablespoon vanilla extract

In a heavy 2- to 3-quart saucepan, heat the cream over moderate heat until bubbles appear around the sides of the pan. Remove the pan from the heat, add the chocolate and stir until it is completely dissolved. Cool to room temperature, stir in the vanilla, and refrigerate the mixture until it is thoroughly chilled.

Pack a 2-quart ice-cream freezer with layers of finely crushed or cracked ice and coarse rock salt in the proportions recommended by the freezer manufacturer. Add cold water if the manufacturer advises it. Then ladle the ice cream into the ice-cream can and cover it.

If you have a hand ice-cream maker, fill it with the ice cream and let it stand for 3 or 4 minutes before beginning to turn the handle. It may take 15 minutes or more of turning for the ice cream to freeze, but do not stop turning at any time or the ice cream my be lumpy.

When the handle can barely be moved, the ice cream is ready to serve or to be molded. If you wish to keep it only for an hour or two, remove the lid and dasher. Scrape the ice cream off the dasher and pack it firmly in the container with a spoon. Cover securely, pour off any water in the bucket and repack the ice and salt solidly around it.

If you have an electric ice-cream maker, fill and cover the can, turn it on and let it churn for about 15 minutes, or until the motor slows or actually stops. Serve the ice cream immediately or follow the procedure above to keep it for an hour or so. Tightly covered, the ice cream may safely be kept in the freezer for several weeks.

To mold the ice cream, pack it tightly into ice-cream or other decorative molds. Fasten the hinges, set a lid on the mold, or cover it tightly with foil. Freeze for 3 or 4 hours, until the ice cream is very firm. Just before serving, wipe the outside of the ice-cream mold with a hot wet towel, open the hinges and carefully turn the ice cream out onto a serving plate. If you have used a conventional mold, dip the bottom briefly into hot water. Invert a serving plate over the mold, grasp plate and mold together firmly, and turn them over, letting the ice cream slide out.

Black-Walnut-and-Honey Ice Cream

To make about 2 quarts

3 egg yolks	2 cups heavy cream
2 cups milk	1 teaspoon vanilla extract
¾ cup honey	2 cups coarsely chopped black
3 egg whites	walnuts

Combine the egg yolks and milk in a heavy 1½- to 2-quart saucepan and beat them with a wire whisk or a rotary or electric beater until the mixture is smooth. Place the pan over low heat, add the honey and, stirring almost constantly, cook for about 10 minutes, or until the custard coats the spoon lightly. (Do not let the custard come anywhere near a boil or it will curdle.) Then pour the custard into a deep bowl and refrigerate for about 1 hour, or until it is thoroughly chilled.

In a separate bowl, beat the egg whites with a wire whisk or a rotary or electric beater until they are stiff enough to form unwavering peaks on the beater when it is lifted from the bowl. With a rubber spatula, incorporate the heavy cream and vanilla into the chilled custard. Scoop the egg whites over the top of the custard mixture and fold them in gently but thoroughly.

Pack a 2-quart ice-cream freezer with layers of finely crushed or cracked ice and coarse rock salt in the proportions recommended by the freezer manufacturer. Add cold water if the manufacturer advises it. Then ladle the ice cream into the ice-cream can and cover it.

If you have a hand ice-cream maker, fill it with the ice cream and let it stand for 3 or 4 minutes before beginning to turn the handle. Then, starting slowly at first, crank continuously for 10 minutes. Do not stop turning at any time or the ice cream may be lumpy.

Add the black walnuts to the ice cream and continue to crank for about 5 minutes longer. When the handle can barely be moved, the ice cream is ready to serve. If you wish to keep it for an hour or two, remove the lid and dasher. Scrape the ice cream off the dasher and pack it firmly in the container with a spoon. Cover securely, pour off any water in the bucket and repack the ice and salt solidly around it.

If you have an electric ice-cream maker, fill and cover the can, turn it on and let it churn for 10 minutes. Turn off the machine, add the black walnuts to the ice cream and let it churn again until the motor slows or actually stops. Serve the ice cream immediately or follow the procedure above to keep it for an hour or two.

Lacking an ice-cream maker, fold the black walnuts into the ice cream and pour the mixture into 3 or 4 ice-cube trays from which the dividers have been removed. Spread the ice cream evenly and smooth the top with a rubber spatula. Freeze for 3 to 4 hours, stirring every 30 minutes and scraping into it the ice particles that form around the edges of the trays.

After the ice cream has been made, it may be covered tightly and kept safely in the freezer for several weeks. Before serving, place the ice cream in the refrigerator for 20 or 30 minutes to let it soften slightly so that it can easily be served.

Cider Pie

To make one 9-inch pie

1½ cups apple cider
1 cup dark brown sugar
2 tablespoons butter, cut into
    ¼-inch bits
¼ teaspoon salt
3 egg yolks
2 egg whites
A 9-inch short-crust sweet pastry
    shell, partially baked and
    cooled *(page 6)*
⅛ teaspoon ground nutmeg,
    preferably freshly grated

In a heavy 2- to 3-quart enameled saucepan, boil the cider uncovered over high heat until it is reduced to ¾ cup. Add the brown sugar, butter bits and salt, and stir until the sugar dissolves and the butter melts. Remove the saucepan from the heat.

Ladle about 2 tablespoons of the hot cider mixture into the egg yolks, mix well with a wire whisk, and then gradually pour the yolks into the cider, whisking all the while.

With a wire whisk or a rotary or electric beater, beat the egg whites until they are stiff enough to stand in unwavering peaks on the beater when it is lifted from the bowl. Scoop the egg whites over the cider mixture and beat them together gently but thoroughly with a wire whisk.

Pour the mixture into the cooled partially baked pie shell and sprinkle the top with the nutmeg. Bake in the middle of the oven for about 30 minutes, or until a knife inserted in the center of the pie comes out clean. Cool the cider pie to room temperature before serving.

Sugar Pie

To make one 9-inch pie

1 cup dark brown sugar
⅓ cup unsifted flour
A 9-inch short-crust sweet pastry
   shell, partially baked and
   cooled *(page 6)*
2 cups light cream
1 teaspoon vanilla extract
2 tablespoons butter, cut into
   ¼-inch bits
½ teaspoon ground nutmeg,
   preferably freshly grated

Preheat the oven to 325°. Combine the brown sugar and flour in a fine sieve and rub them directly into the pie shell with the back of a spoon. Spread the mixture evenly and pat it flat with your fingers or the spoon. Then stir the cream and vanilla together and dribble them slowly over the sugar-flour mixture. Scatter the butter bits on top and sprinkle the pie with the nutmeg.

Bake in the middle of the oven for about 1 hour, or until the top is golden brown and feels firm when prodded gently with a finger. The top of the pie will be lightly filmed with melted butter. Before serving, let the pie cool to room temperature.

Lemon-Soufflé Pie

To make one 9-inch pie

2 egg whites
A pinch of salt
2 egg yolks
¾ cup sugar
¼ cup flour
1 cup milk
¼ cup strained fresh lemon juice
2 teaspoons finely grated fresh
    lemon peel
1 tablespoon butter, melted and
    cooled
A 9-inch short-crust sweet pastry
    shell, partially baked and cooled
    (page 6)

Preheat the oven to 350°. With a wire whisk or a rotary or electric beater, beat the egg whites and salt together until they are stiff enough to
stand in unwavering peaks on the beater when it is lifted from the bowl.

In another bowl, with the same beater, beat the egg yolks lightly. Add
the sugar and flour and, when they are completely incorporated, gradually pour in the milk and lemon juice, beating constantly. Add the lemon
peel and cooled melted butter and beat until the mixture is smooth.

With a rubber spatula, scoop the egg whites over the egg-yolk mixture
and fold them together gently but thoroughly. Continue folding until no
trace of white remains. Pour the mixture into the partially baked pie
shell, spreading it evenly and smoothing the top with the spatula.

Bake in the middle of the oven for 25 to 30 minutes, or until a knife inserted in the center of the pie comes out clean. Cool the lemon-soufflé pie
to room temperature before serving.

Apple-Cheese Pie

To make one 9-inch pie

TOPPING

¾ cup granulated sugar
¾ cup unsifted flour
8 tablespoons butter, chilled and cut
    into ¼-inch bits
½ cup fresh finely grated imported
    Parmesan cheese

Preheat the oven to 375°. To prepare the cheese-and-crumb topping, combine ¾ cup of granulated sugar, ¾ cup of flour and 8 tablespoons of butter bits in a large bowl. Rub the sugar, flour and fat together with your fingertips until they look like flakes of coarse meal. Add the grated cheese and stir until well mixed.

PIE

5 medium-sized tart cooking apples
    (about 1½ pounds), peeled,
    cored and cut lengthwise into
    ⅛-inch-thick slices (about
    5 cups)
1 tablespoon strained fresh lemon
    juice
¼ cup light brown sugar

¼ cup granulated sugar
2 tablespoons flour
1 teaspoon ground cinnamon
¼ teaspoon ground nutmeg
A 9-inch unbaked short-crust sweet
    pastry shell *(page 6)*
1 tablespoon butter, cut into
    ¼-inch bits

Place the apples in a deep mixing bowl, add the lemon juice, and turn the slices about with a spoon to moisten them evenly. Combine the brown sugar, ¼ cup of granulated sugar, 2 tablespoons of flour, the cinnamon and nutmeg and sift them together over the apples. Toss gently but thoroughly with the spoon until the slices are well coated.

Spoon the apple mixture into the unbaked pie shell, spreading it out evenly. Dot the apples with the tablespoon of butter bits and scatter the cheese-and-crumb mixture on top. Bake in the middle of the oven for 40 minutes, or until the topping is golden brown and the apples show no resistance when pierced with the point of a small sharp knife. Let the pie cool to room temperature before serving.

Shoofly Pie

To make one 9-inch pie

1 cup unsifted flour
½ cup light brown sugar
¼ cup vegetable shortening, cut
    into ¼-inch bits
1 teaspoon baking soda
1 cup boiling water
⅔ cup light corn syrup
⅓ cup dark molasses
A 9-inch unbaked short-crust sweet
    pastry shell *(page 6)*

Preheat the oven to 375°. To prepare the crumb topping, combine the flour, brown sugar and shortening in a bowl and rub them together with your fingertips until the mixture resembles coarse meal.

In a deep bowl, dissolve the soda in the boiling water. Then add the corn syrup and molasses, and stir to blend well. Pour the mixture into the unbaked pie shell and sprinkle the crumbs evenly over the top.

Bake the shoofly pie in the middle of the oven for 10 minutes. Reduce the oven temperature to 350° and continue baking for about 25 minutes longer, or until the filling is set and does not quiver when the pie pan is gently shaken from side to side. Do not overbake or the filling will become too dry. Cool the pie to room temperature before serving, and accompany it if you like with sweetened whipped cream or scoops of vanilla ice cream.

Amish Raisin Pie

To make one 9-inch pie

1 cup plus 6 tablespoons sugar
2 tablespoons flour
1 teaspoon salt
2 cups milk
4 egg yolks
2 tablespoons unsalted butter, cut
    into ¼-inch bits

1½ cups coarsely chopped seedless
    raisins
2 teaspoons vanilla extract
A 9-inch short-crust sweet pastry
    shell, fully baked and cooled
    (page 6)
3 egg whites

Combine 1 cup of the sugar, the flour and salt, and sift them together onto a plate or a sheet of wax paper. In a heavy 2- to 3-quart saucepan, heat the milk over moderate heat until bubbles form around the sides of the pan. Remove the pan from the heat and cover to keep the milk warm.

With a wire whisk or a rotary or electric beater, beat the egg yolks in a bowl for a minute or two. Slowly add the sugar-and-flour mixture and continue to beat until the eggs are thick enough to fall in a ribbon when the beater is lifted from the bowl. Add the hot milk in a thin stream, beating all the while. Then pour the mixture back into the saucepan.

Add the butter bits and, stirring deeply into the sides and bottom of the pan with a whisk or a wooden spoon, cook gently over moderate heat for 3 to 5 minutes, until the custard thickens into a smooth heavy cream. Do not let the custard boil at any point but cook it long enough to remove any taste of raw flour.

Remove the pan from the heat, stir in the raisins and vanilla, and pour the custard into the pie shell. Cool to room temperature, cover tightly with foil or plastic wrap and refrigerate for at least 2 hours, or until the custard is firm to the touch.

Preheat the oven to 425°. With a wire whisk or a rotary or electric beater, beat the egg whites until they are stiff enough to stand in unwavering peaks on the beater when it is lifted from the bowl. Beat in the remaining 6 tablespoons of sugar by the spoonful. Scoop the meringue over the custard, then spread it smoothly and make decorative swirls with a metal spatula. Bake the pie in the upper third of the oven for 5 to 10 minutes to brown the meringue lightly.

Serve the pie warm or at room temperature.

Buttermilk Chocolate Cake

To make one 12-by-8-inch cake

CAKE
1 tablespoon butter, softened
½ cup unsweetened cocoa
½ cup boiling water
¾ cup buttermilk
1 tablespoon cider vinegar

1 teaspoon vanilla extract
2 cups unsifted flour
1 teaspoon baking soda
1 teaspoon salt
8 tablespoons (½ cup) lard,
  softened
2 cups dark brown sugar
2 eggs

Preheat the oven to 350°. With a pastry brush, spread the softened butter evenly over the bottom and sides of a 12-by-8-inch shallow baking dish. Mix the cocoa and boiling water to a paste in a small bowl. Cool to lukewarm, then stir in the buttermilk, vinegar and vanilla. Combine the flour, baking soda and 1 teaspoon of salt, and sift them together onto a sheet of wax paper. Set aside.

In a deep bowl, cream the lard and 2 cups of dark brown sugar by beating and mashing them against the sides of the bowl with the back of a spoon until the mixture is light and fluffy. Beat in the eggs, one at a time. Add about 1 cup of the flour mixture and, when it is completely incorporated, beat in about ½ cup of the cocoa mixture. Then add the remaining flour and beat in the rest of the cocoa mixture.

Pour the batter into the buttered dish and bake in the middle of the oven for about 45 minutes, or until a cake tester or toothpick inserted in the center comes out clean. Set the cake aside to cool in the baking dish.

TOPPING
1 cup dark brown sugar
8 tablespoons butter, melted and
  cooled

½ cup heavy cream
A pinch of salt
Confectioners' sugar

When the cake has cooled to room temperature, prepare the topping in the following way: Combine 1 cup of dark brown sugar, the melted cooled butter, cream and a pinch of salt in a bowl and beat vigorously with a spoon until the mixture is smooth. Pour the topping over the cake, spreading it evenly and smoothing the top with a metal spatula. Just before serving, sprinkle the cake lightly with confectioners' sugar and serve it directly from the dish.

Pistachio-Orange Cake

To make one 9-inch 3-layer cake

CAKE

3 tablespoons butter, softened
6 tablespoons plus 2 cups unsifted
  flour
9 egg yolks
1 cup sugar
¼ cup strained fresh orange juice
3 tablespoons finely grated fresh
  orange peel
1 teaspoon orange extract
9 egg whites
¼ teaspoon cream of tartar
1 teaspoon salt

Preheat the oven to 350°. With a pastry brush, spread the 3 teaspoons of softened butter over the bottoms and sides of three 9-inch cake pans. Add 2 tablespoons of flour to each pan and tip the pans from side to side to distribute the flour evenly. Invert the pans and rap the bottoms sharply to remove the excess flour. Set the pans aside.

With a wire whisk or a rotary or electric beater, beat the egg yolks and 1 cup of sugar together for 4 to 5 minutes. When the mixture is thick and fluffy, beat in ¼ cup of orange juice, 3 tablespoons of grated orange peel and the orange extract. Sift in the remaining 2 cups of flour, about ½ cup at a time, beating well after each addition.

In a separate bowl, beat the 9 egg whites, cream of tartar and salt with a wire whisk or a rotary or electric beater until the mixture is thick enough to stand in unwavering peaks on the beater when it is lifted from the bowl. With a rubber spatula, scoop the egg-white mixture over the egg-yolk mixture and fold them together gently but thoroughly.

Pour the batter into the prepared pans, dividing it evenly among them and smoothing the tops with the spatula. Bake in the middle of the oven for 20 to 25 minutes, or until a toothpick or cake tester inserted in the centers comes out clean. Let the cakes cool in the pans for 3 or 4 minutes before turning them out on wire racks to cool completely.

FROSTING

5 egg whites
1½ cups sugar
¾ cup strained fresh orange juice
1 tablespoon white corn syrup
1 tablespoon finely grated fresh
    orange peel
¾ pound butter (24 tablespoons),
    cut into ½-inch bits and
    softened
⅔ cup unsalted pistachios (about
    ¼ pound)

To prepare the frosting, beat 5 egg whites with a wire whisk or a rotary or electric beater until they are stiff enough to stand in firm peaks on the beater when it is lifted out of the bowl. Add ½ cup of sugar and beat until the meringue is smooth. Set aside. Combine the remaining cup of sugar, ¾ cup of orange juice and the corn syrup in a heavy 2- to 3-quart saucepan. Bring to a boil over high heat, stirring until the sugar dissolves. Then cook briskly, uncovered and undisturbed, until the syrup reaches a temperature of 238° on a candy thermometer, or until a drop spooned into ice water immediately forms a soft but compact mass.

Beating constantly, pour the orange syrup into the meringue in a slow, thin stream and continue to beat until the mixture has cooled to room temperature. Add the tablespoon of orange peel, then beat in the butter bits a few pieces at a time.

To assemble the cake, place one cake layer on an inverted 9-inch cake pan and, with a metal spatula, spread about ½ cup of the frosting over it. Add the second layer, frost it, and carefully set the third cake layer in place. Spread the top and sides with the remaining frosting and decorate the cake with the pistachios. Carefully transfer the cake to a serving plate with a large spatula.

Moravian Half-Moons

To make about eighteen ¾-inch-
thick half-moons

CAKE
9 tablespoons butter, softened
2 tablespoons plus 1½ cups
    unsifted flour
1½ teaspoons double-acting
baking powder
½ teaspoon salt
1 cup granulated sugar
3 eggs
¾ cup milk
1 teaspoon vanilla extract

Preheat the oven to 350°. With a pastry brush, spread 1 tablespoon of the softened butter over the bottom and sides of a half-moon cake pan (*opposite*) or a *Rehrücken* pan 13½ inches long, 4½ inches wide and 2½ inches deep. Add 2 tablespoons of the flour and tip the pan from side to side to distribute it evenly. Invert the pan and rap the bottom sharply to remove the excess flour.

Combine the remaining 1½ cups of flour, the baking powder and salt, and sift them together into a bowl. Set aside.

In a deep bowl, cream the remaining 8 tablespoons of softened butter and the cup of granulated sugar by beating and mashing them against the sides of the bowl with the back of a large spoon until the mixture is light and fluffy. Beat in the eggs, one at a time. Add ½ cup of the flour mixture and, when it is well incorporated, beat in ¼ cup of the milk. Repeat two more times, alternating ½ cup of the flour mixture with ¼ cup of milk and beating well after each addition. Stir in the vanilla.

Pour the batter into the buttered and floured pan and bake in the middle of the oven for 35 to 45 minutes, or until a toothpick or cake tester inserted in the center comes out clean. Turn the cake out on a wire rack and let it cool to room temperature.

CHOCOLATE ICING
1½ cups confectioners' sugar
3 tablespoons unsweetened cocoa
3 tablespoons butter, melted and
    cooled
2 to 3 tablespoons milk

Meanwhile, prepare the chocolate and orange icings in the following manner: Combine 1½ cups of confectioners' sugar, the cocoa, 3 tablespoons of cooled melted butter and 2 tablespoons of milk in a bowl. Beat vigorously with a spoon until the mixture is smooth. If the icing seems too thick to spread easily, beat in up to 1 tablespoon more milk, a teaspoonful at a time.

ORANGE ICING
1½ cups confectioners' sugar
4 teaspoons butter, melted and
 cooled

1½ tablespoons finely grated fresh
 orange peel
3 to 4 tablespoons strained fresh
 orange juice

In another bowl, combine 1½ cups of confectioners' sugar, 4 teaspoons of cooled melted butter, the grated fresh orange peel and 3 tablespoons of the orange juice. Beat vigorously with a spoon until the mixture is smooth. If the icing seems thick, beat in up to 1 tablespoon more orange juice, by the teaspoonful.

When the cake has cooled completely, cut it crosswise into slices about ¾ inch thick. Using a metal spatula, spread chocolate icing evenly over half of the top of each slice and orange icing over the other half. Arrange the slices side by side on a plate and serve at once. Or let the slices rest until the icing is dry and glossy, then drape with foil or plastic wrap and set aside at room temperature until ready to serve. The iced slices can safely be kept for 2 or 3 days.

Moravian half-moon cakes must be baked in a long troughlike pan. The traditional pan shown below is an heirloom only a tinsmith could duplicate, but the Austrian *Rehrücken* cake pan may be substituted *(Shopping Guide)*.

Pear Upside-down Cake

To make one 9-inch cake

1 tablespoon butter, softened, plus
    14 tablespoons butter, melted
1 cup light brown sugar
3 medium-sized firm ripe pears
2½ cups unsifted flour
1½ teaspoons baking soda
1 teaspoon ground cinnamon

1 teaspoon ground ginger
¼ teaspoon ground cloves
1 teaspoon salt
½ cup dark molasses
½ cup honey
¾ cup hot water
1 egg
½ cup sugar

Preheat the oven to 350°. With a pastry brush, spread the tablespoon of softened butter evenly on the sides of a 9-inch springform cake pan. Then stir 6 tablespoons of the melted butter and the brown sugar together and pat the mixture smoothly over the bottom of the pan.

Peel the pears with a small sharp knife and cut them in half lengthwise. Scoop out the cores with a small spoon. Then arrange the pear halves in one layer in a heavy 10- to 12-inch skillet and add enough water to cover them by 1 inch. Bring to a boil over high heat, reduce the heat to low, and simmer uncovered for 5 to 10 minutes, until the pears show only slight resistance when pierced with the point of a sharp knife.

With a slotted spoon arrange the pears, cored side down, on a wire rack to drain. To flatten each pear, cut a round slice about ¼ inch thick off the curved side of each half. Place one of the round slices, cut side down, in the center of the sugar-coated pan. Arrange the trimmed halves, core side up, around the round slice so that their stem ends face the center and the pears radiate from it like the spokes of a wheel. Chop the remaining round slices of pear coarsely and set them aside.

Combine the flour, baking soda, cinnamon, ginger, cloves and salt, and sift them together into a bowl. Combine the molasses, honey and hot water in a small bowl and mix together thoroughly.

In a deep bowl, beat the egg and sugar with a large spoon or a wire whisk. Stir in the remaining 8 tablespoons of melted butter. Add about 1 cup of the flour mixture and, when it is thoroughly incorporated, beat in about ½ cup of the molasses-and-honey mixture. Repeat twice, alternating 1 cup of the flour mixture with ½ cup of the molasses-and-honey mixture, and beating well after each addition. Gently stir in the reserved chopped pears and dribble the batter slowly into the pear-lined pan.

Bake in the middle of the oven for about 1½ hours, or until the topping is golden and a toothpick or cake tester inserted in the center comes out clean. Let the cake cool in the pan for about 5 minutes.

To unmold and serve the cake, place an inverted serving plate over the top of the pan. Grasping plate and pan together firmly, turn them over. Rap the plate on a table and the cake should slide out easily. Remove the sides of the pan and serve the cake warm or at room temperature.

Pork Cake

To make one 9-by-5-by-3-inch cake

1 tablespoon butter, softened
¼ pound salt pork, trimmed of all
   rind and cut into ¼-inch dice
½ cup boiling water
2 cups unsifted flour
½ teaspoon baking soda
1 teaspoon ground cinnamon
¼ teaspoon ground allspice

¼ teaspoon ground nutmeg
¼ teaspoon ground cloves
½ cup seedless raisins
½ cup dried currants
⅓ cup (2 ounces) finely diced
   candied citron
1 egg
½ cup sugar
½ cup molasses

Preheat the oven to 300°. With a pastry brush spread 1 tablespoon of the butter over the bottom and sides of a 9-by-5-by-3-inch loaf pan.

Drop the salt pork dice into a small bowl and pour the boiling water over them. Set them aside to soak for 10 or 15 minutes. Combine the flour, baking soda, cinnamon, allspice, nutmeg and cloves, and sift them together into a deep bowl. Add the raisins, currants and citron, and stir to coat them evenly with the flour.

With a wooden spoon, beat the egg, sugar and molasses to a smooth paste. Pour in the pork and its soaking water, and mix well. Then add the flour-and-fruit mixture about ½ cup at a time, beating the batter well after each addition.

Pour the batter into the loaf pan, spreading it evenly and smoothing the top with a rubber spatula. Bake in the middle of the oven for about 1½ hours, or until the top is brown and a toothpick or cake tester inserted in the center comes out clean. Turn the pork cake out on a wire rack and cool to room temperature before serving.

Mother Ann's Birthday Cake

To make one 9-inch 4-layer cake

CAKE

4 tablespoons plus ½ pound
butter, softened
4 tablespoons unsifted flour plus 3
cups flour, sifted before
measuring
½ cup cornstarch

1 tablespoon double-acting baking
powder
1 teaspoon salt
2 cups sugar
1 cup milk
2 teaspoons vanilla extract
12 egg whites

Preheat the oven to 350°. With a pastry brush, spread the 4 tablespoons of softened butter over the bottom and sides of four 9-inch layer-cake pans. Add the 4 tablespoons of unsifted flour and tip the pans from side to side to distribute it evenly. Invert the pans and rap the bottoms sharply to remove the excess flour. Combine the 3 cups of sifted flour, the cornstarch, baking powder and salt, and sift them together into a bowl.

In a deep bowl, cream the remaining ½ pound of softened butter and the sugar by beating and mashing them against the sides of the bowl with the back of a large spoon until the mixture is light and fluffy. Add about 1 cup of the flour mixture and, when it is well incorporated, beat in about ⅓ cup of the milk. Repeat two more times, alternating 1 cup of the flour mixture with ⅓ cup of milk and beating well after each addition. Beat in 2 teaspoons of vanilla.

With a wire whisk or a rotary or electric beater, beat 12 egg whites in a separate bowl until they are stiff enough to stand in unwavering peaks on the beater when it is lifted from the bowl. With a rubber spatula, scoop the egg whites over the batter and fold them together gently.

Pour the batter into the prepared pans, dividing it equally among them and smoothing the tops with the spatula. Bake in the middle of the oven for about 25 minutes, or until a toothpick or cake tester inserted in the centers comes out clean. Let the cakes cool in the pans for 4 or 5 minutes, then turn them out on wire racks to cool completely.

ICING
2 egg whites
1½ cups maple sugar, or substitute
    1½ cups dark brown sugar
⅓ cup water
1 teaspoon vanilla extract

To prepare the icing, beat 2 egg whites with a wire whisk or a rotary or electric beater until they are stiff enough to form unwavering peaks on the beater when it is lifted out of the bowl. Set aside. Combine the maple (or brown) sugar and water in a heavy 2- to 3-quart saucepan. Bring to a boil over high heat, stirring until the sugar dissolves. Then cook briskly, uncovered and undisturbed, until the syrup reaches a temperature of 238° on a candy thermometer or until a drop spooned into ice water immediately forms a soft but compact ball. Remove the pan from the heat.

Beating the egg whites constantly, slowly pour in the hot syrup and continue to beat until the icing mixture is smooth and thick. Beat in 1 teaspoon of vanilla.

FILLING
1½ cups peach preserves, or
    substitute 1½ cups strawberry
    or raspberry jam

To assemble the cake, place one layer on an inverted 9-inch cake pan and, with a metal spatula, spread ½ cup of the fruit preserves or jam over it. Repeat two more times, spreading each cake layer with about ½ cup of the preserves. Carefully set the fourth layer in place and spread the top and sides of the cake with the icing. With a large spatula, transfer the cake to a serving plate.

Applesauce Cake

To make one 9-inch tube cake

APPLESAUCE
3 medium-sized tart cooking apples,
    cored and coarsely chopped
½ cup sugar
2 tablespoons water
2 teaspoons strained fresh lemon
    juice

Combine the apples, ½ cup of sugar, water and lemon juice in a small saucepan and bring to a boil over moderate heat. Reduce the heat to its lowest setting, cover tightly and simmer for 15 to 20 minutes, or until the apples can be easily mashed with the back of a fork. Purée the applesauce through a food mill set over a bowl, or rub it through a fine sieve with the back of a spoon. Then return the purée to the pan and, stirring frequently, cook briskly until the applesauce is thick enough to hold its shape almost solidly in a spoon. Measure 1 cup of the applesauce and set it aside to cool to room temperature.

CAKE
9 tablespoons butter, softened
2 tablespoons plus 2 cups cake flour,
    not the self-rising variety
1 tablespoon unsweetened cocoa
1 teaspoon baking soda
1 teaspoon ground cinnamon
½ teaspoon ground cloves
½ teaspoon salt
1 cup light brown sugar
2 eggs
1 cup coarsely chopped walnuts
½ cup coarsely chopped dates
½ cup seedless raisins

Preheat the oven to 350°. With a pastry brush, spread 1 tablespoon of the softened butter over the bottom and sides of a 9-inch tube pan. Add 2 tablespoons of the flour and tip the pan from side to side to spread it evenly. Then invert the pan and rap the bottom sharply to remove the excess flour. Combine the remaining 2 cups of flour, the cocoa, baking soda, cinnamon, cloves and salt, and sift them together into a bowl or onto a sheet of wax paper. Set aside.

In a deep bowl, cream the remaining 8 tablespoons of softened butter and 1 cup of brown sugar by beating and mashing them against the sides of the bowl with the back of a large spoon until the mixture is light and fluffy. Beat in the eggs, one at a time. Add about ½ cup of the flour-and-cocoa mixture and, when it is thoroughly incorporated, beat in about ¼ cup of the cooled applesauce. Repeat three more times, alternating ½ cup of the flour-and-cocoa mixture with ¼ cup of applesauce and beating well after each addition. When the batter is smooth, stir in the chopped walnuts, the dates and the raisins.

Pour the batter into the tube pan, spreading it and smoothing the top with a rubber spatula. Bake in the middle of the oven for 50 to 60 minutes, or until a cake tester or toothpick inserted in the center comes out clean. Turn the cake out on a rack to cool to room temperature.

ICING
2 cups light brown sugar
8 tablespoons butter, cut into
    ½-inch bits
½ cup heavy cream
1 teaspoon vanilla extract

To prepare the icing, combine 2 cups of brown sugar, 8 tablespoons of butter bits and the cream in a 2- to 3-quart saucepan. Bring to a boil over high heat, stirring until the sugar dissolves. Then cook briskly, uncovered and undisturbed, until the syrup reaches a temperature of 240° on a candy thermometer, or until about ⅛ teaspoon of syrup dropped into ice water immediately forms a soft ball.

Pour the hot syrup into a mixing bowl, add the vanilla, and beat vigorously with a wooden spoon until the mixture is light and creamy. Quickly spread the warm icing on the top and sides of the cake with a metal spatula. If the frosting becomes too stiff as you proceed, dip the spatula into hot water.

Strawberry Spongecake

To make one 9-inch 4-layer cake

1 quart firm ripe strawberries
¾ cup plus 2 tablespoons sugar
2 tablespoons butter, softened
2 tablespoons plus 1 cup unsifted
 flour
A pinch of salt
6 egg whites
6 egg yolks
2 teaspoons vanilla extract
2 cups heavy cream, chilled

Pick over the strawberries, removing the hulls and discarding any blemished berries. Wash the strawberries briefly in a large sieve or colander set under cold running water. Then spread them on paper towels to drain and pat them completely dry with fresh towels.

Select 2 cups of the most attractive berries and set them aside. Drop the remaining berries into a bowl, add ¼ cup of the sugar, and mash the berries to a thick purée by beating them against the sides of the bowl with the back of a spoon. Cover the bowl with foil or plastic wrap and let the puréed strawberries steep at room temperature until ready to serve.

Preheat the oven to 350°. With a pastry brush, spread the softened butter evenly over the bottom and sides of two 9-inch layer-cake pans. Add 1 tablespoon of the flour to each pan and tip it from side to side to spread the flour evenly. Invert the pans and rap their bottoms sharply to remove the excess flour.

Combine the remaining cup of flour and the salt and sift them together onto a plate or a sheet of wax paper. Set aside.

With a wire whisk or a rotary or electric beater, beat the egg whites until they are stiff enough to stand in unwavering peaks on the beater when it is lifted from the bowl. In another bowl and with the same beater, beat the egg yolks, ½ cup of the sugar, and 1 teaspoon of the vanilla together until they are thick and lemon-colored.

Sprinkle the sifted flour and salt over the egg whites, pour the egg-yolk mixture over them and, with a rubber spatula, fold together lightly but thoroughly, using an over-and-under cutting motion rather than a stirring motion.

Pour the batter into the buttered-and-floured pans, dividing it equally among them. Spread the batter and smooth the tops with the spatula. Bake in the middle of the oven for about 20 minutes, or until the cakes begin to shrink away from the sides of the pans and a cake tester or toothpick inserted in the centers comes out clean. Let the cakes cool in the pans for 4 or 5 minutes, then turn them out onto wire racks to cool completely to room temperature.

About half an hour before serving the cake, pour the cream into a large chilled bowl and whip it with a wire whisk or a rotary or electric beater. As soon as the cream becomes frothy, add the remaining 2 tablespoons of sugar and 1 teaspoon of vanilla. Continue to beat until the cream is stiff enough to stand in firm, unwavering peaks on the beater when it is lifted out of the bowl.

To assemble, slice each cake in half horizontally to make four thin layers. Place one of the layers, cut side up, on a serving plate and, with a metal spatula, spread it with about ½ cup of the puréed strawberries. Repeat two more times, spreading the third layer of the cake with all of the remaining puréed berries.

Carefully put the fourth layer on the top, cut side down. Then spread the whipped cream smoothly over the top and sides of the strawberry cake. Cut a dozen or so of the reserved 2 cups of whole strawberries in half lengthwise and set them on the plate, cut side up, in a ring around the cake. Arrange the remaining whole strawberries attractively on the top of the cake and serve at once.

Dried-Apple Cake

To make one 9-inch loaf cake

1 cup dried apples	1 teaspoon ground cinnamon
1 cup dark molasses	½ teaspoon ground cloves
1 tablespoon butter, softened	½ teaspoon salt
2 tablespoons plus 2 cups unsifted flour	1 egg
	1 cup sugar
2 teaspoons baking soda	½ cup sour cream

Starting a day ahead, place the dried apples in a bowl and pour in enough water to cover them by at least 2 inches. Set the apples aside at room temperature to soak overnight.

Drain the apples in a sieve or colander, pat them dry with paper towels and chop them fine. Then combine the chopped apples and molasses in a 2- to 3-quart enameled saucepan and bring to a simmer over moderate heat. Reduce the heat to its lowest setting, cover tightly and simmer for 20 minutes. With a rubber spatula, scrape the entire contents of the pan into a small bowl and set it aside to cool to room temperature.

Preheat the oven to 350°. With a pastry brush, spread the softened butter over the bottom and sides of a 9-by-5-by-3-inch loaf pan. Add 2 tablespoons of the flour and tip the pan from side to side to spread it evenly. Invert the pan and rap the bottom sharply to remove excess flour.

Combine the remaining 2 cups of flour, the baking soda, cinnamon, cloves and salt, and sift them together into a bowl. Set aside.

In a deep bowl, beat the egg, sugar and sour cream together with a wire whisk or a rotary or electric beater until the mixture is thick and smooth. Add the flour mixture, about ½ cup at a time, and beat well after each addition. Then stir in the cooled apple-and-molasses mixture.

Pour the batter into the buttered and floured pan, spreading it evenly and smoothing the top with a rubber spatula. Bake in the middle of the oven for about 1 hour, or until a toothpick or cake tester inserted in the center comes out clean.

Turn the cake out on a wire rack to cool to room temperature. If you like, the dried-apple cake may be served with whipped cream or scoops of vanilla ice cream.

COOKIES

Shaker Aniseed Cookies

To make about 30 diamond-shaped
    cookies

9 tablespoons butter, softened
1½ cups sugar
1 teaspoon aniseed

1 teaspoon vanilla extract
3 eggs
3 cups unsifted flour
1 egg white, lightly beaten
30 whole blanched almonds

In a deep bowl, cream 8 tablespoons of the butter with the sugar by beating and mashing them against the sides of the bowl with the back of a large spoon until the mixture is light and fluffy. Beat in the aniseed and vanilla. Add the eggs, one at a time, beating well after each addition. Then add the flour, about 1 cup at a time, beating well after each addition. Gather the dough into a ball, wrap in wax paper and refrigerate for about 1 hour.

Preheat the oven to 350°. With a pastry brush, spread the remaining tablespoon of softened butter evenly over two large baking sheets. On a lightly floured surface, roll the chilled dough out into a rough rectangle about ½ inch thick. Then, using a ruler and a pastry wheel or a small sharp knife, shape the dough into diamonds by making crisscrossing diagonal cuts 2 inches apart at about a 45° angle. Arrange the cookies an inch apart on the buttered baking sheets. Gather the scraps into a ball, roll them out as before and cut as many more diamond shapes as you can.

Brush the cookies lightly with the egg white and gently press a whole blanched almond into the center of each diamond. Bake in the middle of the oven for 15 to 20 minutes, or until the cookies are firm but not brown. With a metal spatula, transfer the cookies to wire racks to cool. In tightly sealed jars or tins, the Shaker aniseed cookies can safely be stored for several weeks.

Lebkuchen

To make about 5 dozen 2-inch
  square cookies

6 cups unsifted flour
1 tablespoon baking soda
2 teaspoons ground cinnamon
1 teaspoon ground cloves
1 teaspoon ground coriander
1 teaspoon ground nutmeg
2 cups honey or 2 cups light
  molasses
1 cup buttermilk
12 tablespoons (¾ cup) lard,

softened
1 cup sugar
1 egg
½ cup finely chopped candied
  citron
½ cup finely chopped walnuts
1 teaspoon aniseed
4 tablespoons butter, softened
3 cups confectioners' sugar
⅓ cup water

Combine the flour, soda, cinnamon, cloves, coriander and nutmeg, and sift them together onto a sheet of wax paper. Stir the honey or molasses and the buttermilk together in a bowl and set aside.

In a deep mixing bowl, cream the lard and sugar by beating and mashing them against the sides of the bowl with the back of a spoon until the mixture is light and fluffy. Beat in the egg. Add about 1 cup of the flour mixture and, when it is well incorporated, beat in about ½ cup of the buttermilk mixture. Repeat five more times, alternating 1 cup of the flour mixture with ½ cup of the buttermilk mixture and beating well after each addition. Stir in the citron, chopped walnuts and aniseed. Gather the dough into a ball, wrap it in wax paper and refrigerate it for about 1 hour for easier handling.

Preheat the oven to 350°. With a pastry brush, spread 2 tablespoons of the softened butter evenly over two large baking sheets. Cut the dough in half, shape each half into a ball, and return one ball to the refrigerator. Place the remaining ball of dough on a lightly floured surface and roll it out into a rough rectangle about ¼ inch thick.

With a pastry wheel or sharp knife, cut the dough into 2-inch squares and arrange the squares about 1 inch apart on the buttered baking sheets. Bake in the middle of the oven for 12 to 15 minutes, or until the *lebkuchen* are firm to the touch.

With a spatula, slide the cookies onto wire racks. Stir the confectioners' sugar and water to a smooth paste and brush a little of the mixture over the tops of the *lebkuchen* while they are still warm.

Let the baking sheets cool completely, then spread them with the remaining 2 tablespoons of softened butter. Roll out the second ball of cookie dough as before. Following the identical procedure, cut and bake the remaining *lebkuchen,* and glaze them with the rest of the confectioners'-sugar-and-water paste. In a tightly covered jar or tin, the *lebkuchen* can safely be kept for 2 or 3 weeks.

Walnut Crescents

To make about 4 dozen cookies

2 tablespoons butter, softened, plus
½ pound butter, chilled and cut
into ¼-inch bits, plus 3
tablespoons butter, melted
¾ cup light brown sugar
1½ teaspoons ground cinnamon

¾ cup finely chopped walnuts
1 cup (8 ounces) creamed cottage
cheese
2 cups flour, sifted before
measuring
1 egg yolk, lightly beaten with 2
tablespoons cold water

Preheat the oven to 400°. With a pastry brush, spread the 2 tablespoons of softened butter evenly over two large baking sheets. Combine the brown sugar and cinnamon and sift them together into a bowl. Add the chopped nuts and mix well. Set aside.

Place the cottage cheese and ½ pound of the butter bits in a deep bowl and mash them together with a large spoon. Add the flour, stir briefly, then rub the flour and fat between your fingers until they are well blended and the dough can be gathered into a ball. Cut the dough into three equal parts and shape each part into balls.

To shape the cookies, place one ball of dough on a lightly floured surface and roll it out into a circle about 10 inches in diameter and ⅛ inch thick. Brush the circle with 1 tablespoon of the melted butter and sprinkle the top evenly with ½ cup of the brown-sugar-and-walnut mixture. Using a small sharp knife or a pastry wheel, cut the circle into quarters, then into eighths, and finally into 16 wedges. Starting from the wide outside edge, roll up each wedge and shape the roll into a crescent. Arrange the crescents 1 inch apart on the baking sheet, then roll and shape each of the remaining balls of dough in a similar fashion.

With the pastry brush, coat the top and sides of each crescent lightly with the egg-yolk-and-water mixture. Bake in the middle of the oven for 12 to 15 minutes, or until the crescents are golden brown. Then transfer them to wire racks to cool before serving. In a tightly covered jar, the walnut crescents can safely be kept for 2 or 3 weeks.

Moravian Sand Tarts

To make about 8 dozen medium-
   sized cookies

3½ cups flour, sifted before
   measuring
2 teaspoons double-acting baking
   powder
1 teaspoon salt
½ pound plus 4 tablespoons
   butter, softened

2⅓ cups sugar
3 eggs
1 teaspoon vanilla extract
2 teaspoons ground cinnamon
1 cup very finely chopped walnuts
½ cup milk

Combine the flour, baking powder and salt, and sift them together onto a plate or a sheet of wax paper.

In a deep bowl, cream ½ pound of the softened butter with 2 cups of the sugar, beating and mashing the mixture against the sides of the bowl with the back of a spoon until it is light and fluffy. Beat in the eggs, one at a time and, when they are well incorporated, stir in the flour mixture by the cupful. Add the vanilla and continue to beat until the dough is smooth. Cover with wax paper or plastic wrap and refrigerate the dough for at least 8 hours, or overnight.

Preheat the oven to 350°. With a pastry brush, spread 1 tablespoon of the remaining softened butter evenly over two large baking sheets. Mix the remaining ⅓ cup of sugar, the cinnamon and nuts together and set them aside.

Cut off about one quarter of the dough and shape it into a ball. (Return the rest to the refrigerator.) On a lightly floured surface, roll the ball of dough out into a rough circle about ⅛ inch thick. Cut the dough into any shapes you like, using a star, heart or other decorative cookie cutter. Gather the scraps together into a ball and roll out as before. Then cut as many more cookies as you can. Brush the tops of the cookies lightly with milk and sprinkle them with a little of the sugar-and-nut mixture.

With a wide metal spatula, arrange the sand tarts about 1 inch apart on the baking sheets. Bake in the middle of the oven for 8 to 10 minutes, or until the cookies are crisp around the edges and the tops feel firm when prodded gently with a finger. With the spatula, transfer the sand tarts to wire racks to cool.

Let the baking sheets cool completely, then repeat the entire procedure three more times—using 1 tablespoon of the softened butter to grease the pans for each batch of cookies and rolling and baking one quarter of the dough at a time. In a tightly covered jar or box, the Moravian sand tarts can safely be kept for 2 or 3 weeks.

Moravian Animal Cookies

To make about 8 dozen medium-
  sized cookies

3 cups unsifted flour	4 tablespoons lard, softened
1 teaspoon ground ginger	½ cup sugar
½ teaspoon salt	1 cup dark molasses
8 tablespoons butter, softened	1 tablespoon rum

Combine the flour, ginger and salt, and sift them together onto a plate or a sheet of wax paper.

In a deep bowl, cream 4 tablespoons of the softened butter, the lard and sugar, beating and mashing the mixture against the sides of the bowl with the back of a spoon until it is light and fluffy. Beat in about 1 cup of the flour mixture and, when it is well incorporated, add about ⅓ cup of the molasses. Repeat two more times, alternating 1 cup of the flour mixture with ⅓ cup of molasses and beating well after each addition. Stir in the rum, cover the bowl with wax paper or plastic wrap, and refrigerate the dough for at least 8 hours, or overnight.

Preheat the oven to 350°. With a pastry brush, spread 1 tablespoon of the remaining softened butter evenly over the two large baking sheets.

Cut off about one quarter of the dough and shape it into a ball. (Return the rest to the refrigerator.) On a lightly floured surface, roll the ball of dough out into a rough circle about ⅛ inch thick.

Cut the dough into animal shapes with animal cookie cutters. Gather the scraps together into a ball and roll out as before. Then cut as many more animal cookies as you can.

With a wide metal spatula, arrange the animal cookies about 1 inch apart on the baking sheets. Bake in the middle of the oven for 5 to 8 minutes, or until the tops feel firm when prodded gently with a finger. With the spatula, transfer the cookies to wire racks to cool.

Let the baking sheets cool completely, then repeat the entire procedure three more times—using 1 tablespoon of the softened butter to grease the pans for each batch of animal cookies and rolling and baking one quarter of the dough at a time.

In a tightly covered jar or box, the Moravian animal cookies can safely be kept for 2 or 3 weeks.

Tom Thumb Cookies

To make about 3 dozen 2-by-1-inch
   cookies

BOTTOM LAYER
9 tablespoons butter, softened
½ cup dark brown sugar
1 cup flour, sifted before measuring

Preheat the oven to 325°. With a pastry brush, spread 1 tablespoon of the butter over the bottom and sides of a shallow 13-by-9-inch baking dish and set it aside.

In a deep bowl, cream the remaining 8 tablespoons of butter with ½ cup of dark brown sugar by beating and mashing them against the sides of the bowl with the back of a large spoon until the mixture is light and fluffy. Beat in 1 cup of sifted flour, a few tablespoonfuls at a time.

With a rubber spatula, scrape the mixture into the buttered baking dish and spread it evenly over the bottom of the dish with the spatula or your fingers. Bake in the middle of the oven for 15 minutes.

TOP LAYER
2 eggs
1 teaspoon vanilla extract
1 cup dark brown sugar
2 tablespoons flour
½ teaspoon double-acting baking
   powder
A 3½-ounce can moist shredded
   coconut
1 cup finely chopped walnuts
Confectioners' sugar

Meanwhile, in a deep bowl, beat the eggs and vanilla with a wire whisk or a rotary or electric beater until they begin to froth. Add 1 cup of dark brown sugar and continue beating for 4 or 5 minutes longer, or until the mixture is thick enough to fall in a slowly dissolving ribbon when the beater is lifted from the bowl. Combine the 2 tablespoons of flour and the baking powder, sift them together over the egg mixture, and mix well. Add the coconut and walnuts and fold them gently into the batter with a rubber spatula.

When the cake has baked its allotted time, remove the dish from the oven and let it cool for a minute or so. Then, pour the coconut batter on top, spreading it evenly and smoothing it with the spatula. Bake for about 20 minutes, or until the topping is golden brown.

Cool to room temperature, then sprinkle the top lightly with confectioners' sugar and cut the cake into 2-by-1-inch cookies.

Recipe Index

NOTE: Size, weight and material are specified for pans in the recipes because they affect cooking results. A pan should be just large enough to hold its contents comfortably. Heavy pans heat slowly and cook food at a constant rate. Aluminum and cast iron conduct heat well but may discolor foods containing egg yolks, wine, vinegar or lemon. Enamelware is a fairly poor conductor of heat. Many recipes therefore recommend stainless steel or enameled cast iron, which do not have these faults.

Photographs on pages 4 and 5 by Walter Daran; photographs on pages 30 and 31 by Costa Manos; photograph on page 135 by Richard Jeffery. Illustrations, based on designs on an early American chest, are from *American Folk Decoration* by Jean Lipman with Eve Meulendyke, Oxford University Press.

Soups

Chicken-corn soup 15
Clam bisque 13
Consommé Bellevue 12
Dried-mushroom soup 16
Manhattan clam chowder 14
Philadelphia pepper pot 10
Philadelphia snapper soup 11
Shaker herb soup 12
Shaker potato-leek soup 9
Wild elderberry soup 8

Vegetables and Salads

Batter-fried mushrooms 17
Broccoli purée 20
Cauliflower with buttered crumbs 25
Celery slaw 26
Corn custard 21
Fresh asparagus with lemon cream sauce,
    Shaker style 19
Fresh spinach and herbs, Shaker style 20
Mushroom-stuffed potatoes 24
Potato filling 22
Sautéed potato balls 23
Shaker salad 26
Summer squash soufflé 18
Waldorf salad 27

Meat

Barbecued venison chops 38
Beef potpie 34
Braised pork chops 28
Creamed chipped beef in toasted
    bread cups 43
Deviled short ribs 33
Flank steak with meat stuffing,
    Shaker style 32
Indiana farm sausage 41
Martha Washington's "grand leg
    of lamb" 36
Pasties, Michigan style 30
Pigs' feet souse 35
Pot-roasted loin of pork 29
Schnitz und kneppe 42
Smoked pork chops and lentils 31
Stuffed fresh ham 44
Sweetbreads *en coquille* 40
Venison stew 39

Poultry and Game Birds

Batter-fried chicken 49
Braised pheasant with sauerkraut 55
Braised wild duck 58

Broiled quail with mustard butter 61
Chicken breasts and ham with sherried
   cream sauce 46
Chicken croquettes 50
Chicken mousse 48
Chicken potpie 47
Chicken Stoltzfus 52
Chicken-stuffed onions, Shaker style 45
Roast duck with apricot-rice stuffing 60
Roast pheasant with filbert stuffing and
   currant sauce 56
Stewed chicken with parsley dumplings 53

Fish and Shellfish

Barbecued stuffed coho salmon 66
Batter-fried bluegills 62
Broiled bluefish fillets 76
Broiled skewered scallops 76
Clam fritters 74
Clam tart 75
Fried lake perch fillets with tartar sauce 63
John Clancy's broiled clams 73
Lobster croquettes 77
Lobster thermidor 78
Mushroom-stuffed halibut steak 64
New York oyster stew 70
Oysters casino 72
Philadelphia baked clams 70
Planked shad with potatoes *duchesse* 68
Poached salmon steaks with mousseline sauce 65
Shad roe on a bed of sorrel 69
Steamer clams remoulade 71

Breads, Biscuits and Breakfast Cakes

Apple muffins 94
Blueberry muffins 95
Buttermilk soda biscuits 91
Cornmeal griddle cakes 85
Cottage-cheese pancakes 97
Dilly bread 82
Fastnachts 101
Fried yeast biscuits 90
Funnel cakes 93
Moravian sugar cake 100
Philadelphia cinnamon buns 96
Potato bread 83
Pumpkin bread 89
Salt-rising bread 86
Schwenkfelder cake 98
Sour-cream cornbread 80
Sugar doughnuts 92
Wild-persimmon and hickory-nut bread 81
Whole-wheat bread 87

Pickles, Preserves and Relishes

Apple butter 107
Bread-and-butter pickles 103
Chowchow 104
Crab-apple jelly 106
Ground-cherry jam 106
Pennsylvania Dutch coleslaw 110
Pennsylvania pepper relish 108
Pepper cabbage 110
Red beet eggs 109
Spiced cantaloupe 108

Nuts

Mixed-nut brittle 113
Sherried walnuts 112
Spiced mixed nuts 111
Toasted pecans 112

Desserts

Amish raisin pie 130
Apple-cheese pie 128
Apple Jonathan 114
Applesauce cake 140
Black-walnut-and-honey ice cream 124
Blueberry crumb cake 122
Buttermilk chocolate cake 131
Chocolate ice cream 123
Cider pie 125
Cracker pudding 121
Dried-apple cake 144
Floating island 118
Indiana persimmon pudding 119
Lemon rice pudding 120
Lemon-soufflé pie 127
Moravian half-moons 134
Mother Ann's birthday cake 138
Peach custard 115
Pear upside-down cake 136
Pistachio-orange cake 132
Pork cake 137
Raspberry cream roll 116
Shoofly pie 129
Strawberry flummery 117
Strawberry spongecake 142
Sugar pie 126

Cookies

Lebkuchen 146
Moravian animal cookies 149
Moravian sand tarts 148
Shaker aniseed cookies 145
Tom Thumb cookies 150
Walnut crescents 147

XXX Printed in U.S.A.